PROCLAIMING THE TRUTH

Guides to Scriptural Preaching

PROCLAIMING THE TRUTH

Guides to Scriptural Preaching

Donald E. Demaray

**Evangel
Publishing House**
Nappanee, Indiana

Toll-free Order Line: (800) 253-9315
Internet Website: www.evangelpublishing.com

First edition published by Baker Book House, Grand Rapids, Michigan, 1979, ISBN 0-8010-2898-1.

Biblical quotations, unless otherwise noted, are from the New Revised Standard Version Bible, copyright 1989, by the Division of Christian Education of the National Council of the Churches of Christ in the USA, and are used by permission.

Cover Design: Ted Ferguson
Index: Glen A. Pierce

Demaray, Donald E.
      Proclaiming the truth : guides to scriptural preaching / Donald E. Demaray
– 2nd ed.
      p. cm.
      Includes bibliographical references and index.
      LCCN: 00-111057
      ISBN 10: 1-928915-17-5
      ISBN 13: 978-1-928915-17-1

      1. Preaching–Handbooks, manuals, etc. 2. Bible–Homiletical use. I. Title.

BV4211.3.D46 2001 251
               QBI01-200158

Printed in the United States of America
07 08 09 10 11 EP 9 8 7 6 5

For Jodi

Faithful Preacher of God's Word

Contents

Foreword ix

Preface xiii

1. William Barclay's Principles: Technique 1

2. William Barclay's Principles (Continued) 15

3. Interpretation: How to Determine Meanings 39

4. Integration: Putting It All Together 53

5. Authority: Three Crucial Components 73

Appendix: 100 Books for the Preacher's Library 85

Bibliography 99

Index 115

Foreword

I like what Robert Frost said about how poems came to him. He never succeeded in "larruping a poem like one might a horse to make it go," but rather, "a poem begins with a lump in the throat; a homesickness, or a lovesickness. It is the reaching out toward expression; an effort to find fulfillment. A complete poem is where an emotion has found its thought, and the thought has found the words."[1]

Doesn't that have the feel of John about it? "What we have heard, have seen with our eyes have looked upon and touched with our hands . . . we proclaim to you" (1 John 1:1-2). And doesn't it vibrate with the emotion of Paul? "For what we preach is not ourselves, but Jesus Christ as Lord" (2 Cor. 4:5).

That's not everything preaching is, but it is at least that: an emotion that has found its thought and a thought that has found its word. So the word is important. That's a gross understatement, but I don't know any other way to say it. Words are powerful, creative, life-changing. Words make things happen.

Donald Demaray knows that. His conviction that words are powerful, creative and life-changing has shaped his vocation. For all of his ministry years, he has given priority to preaching. For nearly thirty-four years, his vocation has had the sharp focus of teaching young women and men the art and science of proclaiming the Word of God. And that's what this book is about.

Don is an excellent writer, putting words together in a way that makes sense—precise, clear and logical. But he knows with Socrates that the spoken word is sharper than the written word. "I would rather write upon the hearts of living men than upon the skins of dead sheep," the ancient Greek philosopher said. It may be a bit inelegant to quote Adolph Hitler in the same context as Socrates, but we need to remember that he was famous for his ruthless

---

[1]Quoted in Robert Frost, *A Tribute to the Source* (New York: Holt, Rinehart and Winston, 1979), 105.

realism, far more interested in results than petty theories. In *Mein Kampf*, that strange collection of lies, half-truths, keen insights and neurotic madness, Hitler wrote, "I know that one is able to win people far more by the spoken word than by the written word, and that every great movement on this globe owes its rise to the great speakers and not to the great writers."[2]

Words do make things happen. For that reason, this book is very important.

In the United States every Sunday, more than two hundred and fifty thousand sermons are being preached. Since worship on Sunday morning is the primary experience with the Word of God on the part of most Christians, it seems ludicrous even to ask a question about the importance of preaching. Yet that question gets raised now and again. Opinion-makers in the church have told us from time to time that preaching is irrelevant. They have insisted that some form of ministry other than preaching would be more effective in accomplishing what the church is about. First, it was Christian eduction; then it was counseling; then it was social action; then it was small groups. (I'm not sure it was all in that order, but you know what I am talking about.) Interestingly, the laity neverallowed themselves to become sidetracked in that fashion. Ask the laity what they see as the primary task of their minister. The answer will always include a statement something like this: "We want a person who can preach and who cares about people."

It is my conviction—and certainly one shared by Donald Demaray—that little if anything else we do as pastors and preachers, or that anyone else does for that matter, is more important than authentic preaching. It's difficult to imagine the continuation of the church or of the Christian faith without preaching.

This book is about authentic preaching. The thesis of this book is that, if preaching is worth doing, it's worth doing well. It's worth investing our best energy and a huge amount of our time. It should be **the top priority of our ministry agenda as pastors and preachers**.

---

[2]Both Socrates and Hitler quoted in Earl Kennedy, *His Word Through Preaching* (New York: Harper and Brothers Publishers, 1947), 11, 17.

In a succinct but rather comprehensive way, Donald Demaray introduces the principles and techniques of master homileticians. Thus, he provides worthy guides for persons who wish to enhance their effectiveness in proclaiming the truth. The how-to of sermon development (clarifying ideas, focusing the message, outlining the thoughts, making relevant the Scripture, integrating various dimensions of the truth, contextualizing the text, making it all practical and relevant) is all here in an easy-to-use presentation.

But there is more. Early on, the necessity of a preacher's compulsion to preach is underscored. Effective communicators must burn with a passion to preach. There's also the call to integrity—the harmony of preaching with the life of the preacher. A clear and forceful challenge to biblical preaching dominates the entire presentation.

This book affirms what one of my preacher heroes, Bishop Gerald Kennedy, taught me years ago: that preaching is not merely education (though any self-respecting preacher certainly aims at educating the congregation, since this is part of the preacher's function). Preaching is not the delivery of an essay in which one gives comments on life and passing events, though we can hardly preach without doing this. It is not a theological lecture, though the sermon must contain theology and should be theologically sound. The sermon is not a discussion of morals, though it will not lack moral teaching. It's not just a discussion of political or social matters. Preaching is not an effort to urge a particular program of reform, though we preachers cannot keep silent when a moral choice stands before our people. No, preaching is not any of these things. Preaching is our witnessing to the Word of God.

Bishop Kennedy concluded his warning about what preaching is not: "Our danger is that we will see ourselves as mere agents of an institution or promoters of a vested interest. In the final analysis, we are not employees at all, but unworthy voices of the Living God, who 'hath at the end of these days spoken unto us in His Son.'....The preacher is not just a [person] with some ideas to proclaim about God or some information to impart concerning a philosophy of life.

[The preacher] is the agent through whom God probes and challenges...the voice through which God shows himself as a consuming fire, and offers himself as a very present help in time of trouble through Jesus Christ. Preaching is confronting man's tragic inadequacy with God's redeeming grace."[3]

So the principles and techniques of preaching, as Donald Demaray shares them, are rooted and grounded in the eternal purpose of preaching, that "the Word might become flesh and live again."

You can't read this book without wanting to be a better preacher. If you appropriate the content of it, you will be a better preacher.

You can't read this book without having your passion to preach revived, without feeling that fire burning in your bones, which may have been what brought you to this vocation in the first place: "Woe is me if I do not preach the gospel."

I can't think long about preaching (and certainly can't read a book such as this about preaching) without recalling a word of Bishop William A. Quayle. Back in 1910, he wrote a book entitled, *The Pastor-Preacher*, in which he described the person who has exercised faithfully the vocation as preacher.

> When this preacher comes to a Sunday in his journey through the week, people ask him, "Preacher-man, where are you and what saw you while the workadays were sweating at their toil?" And then of this preacher we may say reverently, "He opened his mouth and taught them, saying"; and there will be another though lesser Sermon on the Mount. And the auditors sit and sob and shout under their breath, and say with their helped hearts, "Preacher, saw you and heard you that? You were well employed. Go out and listen and look another week; but be very sure to come back and tell us what you heard and saw."[4]

This book will help you be that kind of preacher.

Maxie D. Dunnam, President
Asbury Theological Seminary

[3]Kennedy, *His Word Through Preaching*, 8.
[4]William A. Quayle, *The Pastor-Preacher* (Cincinnati: Jennings & Graham, 1910), 310.

Preface

Richard Baxter, that seventeenth-century preacher who never knew if he would leave the pulpit alive, so ill was he, cried, "I preach as never sure to preach again. And as a dying man to dying men."

Yet here's the problem: we tend not to take preaching seriously. Joe sat in my preaching course for three weeks, then one day as we left the classroom at the end of a period, he startled me by saying, "I never knew anyone could get so enthusiastic about preaching as you." His unbelieving tone coupled with his look of astonished wonder led me to believe Joe had never heard solid, imaginative, biblical preaching. I have had such students all my life, students who grew up in churches never hearing either the historical or spiritual facts of Scripture. Sermons that do not bring people to points of decision and genuine spiritual formation, do not originate in the heart of God, do not come from the hearts of urgent preachers. My heart cries for pulpit people who herald the mighty acts of God and cry out against the sins that plague us.

Pretty essays from the pulpit will not do the job, a recap of current events will not do the job. Urgent proclamation will change lives. When we preachers really believe what we talk about, we will see changed lives. Conviction marks the truly biblical preacher. Perhaps Joe's preachers did not believe what they preached.

Focus on the needs of the individuals in the pew will let us know they do not want a fairy tale but the genuine, believable article. Think, then, of the needs of your people when you prepare to enter the pulpit next Sunday. A father has heard the ominous words, "You have melanoma." A single young woman knows she's pregnant; should she marry? Another suffered an accident and broke one if not two vertebrae. (I choose actual examples here.) Do you have a word to say to these hurting people? The Bible, above all books, can provide strength and comfort.

Reflect too on the victories and successes of your people. A scout has earned his Eagle award after enormous effort and careful planning. A couple have become parents for the first time; both baby and mother do well. A businessman got an unexpected promotion. Do you have an appropriate word of affirmation for such as these? The Bible contains more affirmative declarations than anyone can count.

You must also come to terms with the complacent, those who attend church, at least now and then, but really do not expect anything very grand. Alexander Pope had a word for such unbelievers: "Blessed are those who expect nothing, for they will never be disappointed." How can you stir up the lethargic? The Bible can do it. Preach the Word! Mind you, the unexpectants may not come alive all at once, but never forget Billy Graham's cogent and very true words, "Wherever the Gospel is preached, no matter how crudely, there are bound to be results."

St. Paul readily confessed that "God was pleased through the foolishness of what was preached to save those who believe" (1 Cor. 1:21). But a sure word from the Lord will speak, sooner or later, to the hurting, to the victorious, to the complacent.

Problem-solving preaching can, of course, become humanistic; answers sought from our own wants instead of God's will. The threat here relates to over-much emphasis on research and secular commentary instead of due focus on God's Word

Some parishioners squirm when the preacher actually touches their lives where they are. To touch people with the living truth that restores hope and vigor for life—well! that makes any homiletical effort worthwhile. To remind parishioners of the moral standard, its authority in God's Word, renews security. To show that God is the rescuer of persons struggling for air amidst the swirling, changing waters of life brings a strong sense of security. To let them know God does indeed meet actual needs, and to demonstrate how to open doors to receive help—that service makes the angels in heaven sing praise.

To help you get through to your people, at whatever level of need, I have done commentary in this book on William Barclay's principles of preaching. I dedicate the first two chapters to those principles. Some comments loom so important—for example, the power of picture preaching—that I pick up those ideas for still further elaboration here and there in the remainder of the book. I attempt further to lay the ground for elementary concerns about interpreting the Bible, and go on to answer the ever-present question, How do I put together a sermon that communicates? Then comes the conclusion to the book with focus on the all-important concern about authority in the pulpit.

Subsequent to the final chapter, I offer a list of one hundred books with alternative suggestions, for the preacher's library. I also suggest a website, and indicate where others can be found.

Many deserve notes of credit. To my faithful secretaries Laurie Verry and Tracy Hoffman, I owe a special debt of gratitude. My in-house editor, my wife Kathleen, labors over my prose with diligence. Harold Burgess, longtime friend, introduced me to Evangel Publishing House. Glen Pierce, patient encourager, editor at Evangel, knows how to inspire a writer. Joe Allison, acquaintance of many years, became publishing manager for Evangel as this book went to press and we again had an opportunity to share the joy of Christian publishing.

How does a writer say thank you to dozens of students who have asked probing questions and made genuinely careful observations? How does one express gratitude to colleagues, seminary and college professors, along with administrators? The many who have contributed to my publications, I simply cannot name for lack of space.

Donald E. Demaray
Spring 2001
Asbury Theological Seminary

1

William Barclay's Principles:
Technique

The renewal of preaching in our day, if it comes, will spring
from knowing the Scriptures and the power of God and not
from new-found skills in titillating the topical.
—David H.C. Read, *Sent From God*, p. 105

Arouse interest, secure favor, and prepare to lead.
—Cicero

William Barclay, widely considered Scotland's most popular
preacher at the height of his career, preached the gospel for over half
a century. He died at age seventy of Parkinson's disease in 1978.
Over time he came to firm conclusions about preaching. These
principles, hammered out on the anvil of desk preparation and
pulpit experience, spell out in simple and basic form eminently
useful tools.[1]

A great deal of the effect of preaching depends on technique.

Barclay develops his first principle with a delightful example
from the culinary art. Two cooks use the same ingredients; one produces a most tasty dish, the other "a revolting and uneatable mess."
The difference lies in technique.

---

[1]William Barclay, *William Barclay: A Spiritual Autobiography* (Grand Rapids:
William B. Eerdmans, 1975).

The vivid analogy reminds us that we all use the same ingredients: biblical materials, illustrations, Christian doctrines, church traditions. Creative preachers come up with interesting, meaty and inspirational sermons; other ministers serve dull dishes.

The challenge is not merely to develop techniques, but the most effective techniques. We aim at mastering techniques for capturing the best ideas, gathering the most interesting data, arranging materials into memorable sequences, starting sermons with captivating issues, and concluding messages with driving urgency. Moreover, we want the best oral methods to insure both audible and winsome public speech, including acceptable English, apt word selection, and creative phrasing for clear and engaging communication. Body language, too, enters the picture; bodily action that appeals to the eye and expresses the intended message.

We face, then, four areas of challenge: (a) homiletics, (b) linguistics, (c) tonetics, and (d) kinesics (body language).

Homiletics

Homiletics, both an art and a science, refers specifically to pulpit communication. It relates to the crucial question every preacher encounters: How do I get through to my people? The very term "homiletics" relates to words like *conversation*, *affable*, *gathering*, *company*—all of which suggest making contact with the audience.

How then do we effect contact? First, we do it by **focusing**. Focus is the genius of communication. Isolating the clear and central truth of the text from which the sermon will come constitutes the preacher's primary preparation task. What *one* truth, not two or three truths, do I want to share?[2]

Put that single sermon thesis at the top of your sermon: The purpose of this sermon is…. Then, as the sermon unfolds, all concerns will relate to that singular purpose.

Now we stand ready to do what we call **mapping**. A good homiletician is a good cartographer, viewing the landscape of the

---

[2]Consider John Henry Jowett's classic statement, "I am of the conviction that no sermon is ready for preaching, nor ready for writing out, until we can express its theme in a short, pregnant sentence as clear as a crystal." See Jowett's *The Preacher, His Life and Work* (Grand Rapids: Baker Book House reprint, 1968), p. 133.

preaching passage from the Bible, noting the outline of the oceans, observing the mountain peaks, and taking notice of the valleys.

Once the map comes into view, then ask, "How do I get from the overall picture to the goal of my sermon?" If I wish to travel from Cincinnati, Ohio to Atlanta, Georgia, I find Interstate 75 on the map and follow it to my destination. I refuse side trips, interesting though they may appear. I stick to I-75.

Sticking to my road is the secret of helping my people listen. And just there I come to grips with my pulpit task. I assist my audience in the grand enterprise of hearing the gospel. I cannot make the people listen; nor can I manipulate them into receptivity. Certainly I cannot confuse them, or they will opt out of the listening venture entirely. The bottom line: I help create an environment of attentiveness by focusing on a single subject and mapping the route to that subject goal, veering not to the left nor to the right.

When the sermon map has come to completion, either by classical outlining, or by doing some other kind of sequencing, one must ask, How will I launch this homily? **Getting started** has a lot to do with one's success in capturing the attention of the audience and holding it. Shaping the introduction can make or break a pulpit presentation.

Olympic swimmers have discovered a key to winning: the swimmers who hit the water farthest out have a distinct advantage. Photographs of water athletes' entrances into the pool document their likelihood of coming off with or without the prize medals. So get a good start!

Brevity marks the best starters. Dive in all at once, giving no more than two or three minutes to opening remarks. Then get on with the body of the sermon. Divers do not linger at the beginning of the contest; of necessity, they swim for all their worth, getting on with the meet. Just so with preaching. Capture the attention of your audience, then get on with the body of the sermon.

We move now to **transitioning**, building bridges between the segments of your sermon body. Suppose you have three great movements to your homily. You know what you want to say to make clear the A section, the B section and finally the C section. You must now determine how you will build bridges between A, B, and C. Sometimes, simple transitional statements will do the job. Examples:

- •We have come now to the second division of our sermon.
- •Having come one step, we go on to a second.
- •Our first concern pointed to King David, the second directed us to King Saul, the final consideration brought to mind King Solomon.

Not all sermons fall into such neatly outlined patterns; some simply follow a story trail. But the plot line of the narrative will have its pauses, and often runway sentences to guide both the preacher and the audience to follow the unfolding of the account.

That leads us to a major consideration, **pictorializing**. And here we must spend some time. We live in a telecommunications world. People, conditioned to screens and TV sets, think in pictures. We play games on televisions and computers. Magazines publish high-definition graphics alongside eye-appealing formatted print material. Newspapers fill with photographs. The bottom line: the culture thinks in pictures. So much so that the most fundamental law of communication is just this: *people do picture thinking.*

If, for example, I announce at the outset of a sermon on salvation that I intend to preach on "Justification by Faith," people automatically turn down their hearing aids. If, on the other hand, I begin my sermon on this highly important subject with the true story of George, an alcoholic for 13 years who tried 13 cures and failed at each, immediately I have the attention of my people.

So depressed did George become that he determined to take his life. In preparation for suicide, he visited a Salvation Army thrift shop to buy a suit so the authorities would find his body in clean clothes. Ready to purchase the fresh set of clothes from the nice lady behind the checkout desk, he heard her say, "In a few minutes we will have a worship service in the building next door. Would you like to stay to hear Major Phil Needham? He's a fine speaker." George saw no reason to say no, entered the worship hall, and heard the Major who, at the close of his sermon, invited people to come to the penitent form (kneeling altar) to seek God. George went forward, found Christ, and to make a long story short, experienced a complete cure of his alcohol addiction.

When George told me that story, he had served as a Salvation Army minister for some 13 years. I call George my 13, 13, 13 friend: 13 years an alcoholic, 13 cures that failed, and 13 years in gospel ministry.

What happened to George? God saved him: saved him as a person, saved him from suicide, saved him from a debilitating habit, saved him for Christian ministry. The story paints a vivid picture full of liberation and real-life drama. Clearly the account makes salvation come to life.

Brain studies in our time give us clues about how human beings respond to communication efforts. We talk about right brain and left brain capabilities. The right brain relates to imaginative material like narrative, pictures, the arts, poetry, and feeling and relational matters.

Right Brain Functions

- *Imaging*
- *Poetry*
- *Pictures*
- *Feeling*
- *Relational Experiences*

Left brain functions include analytical, logical, systematic kinds of activities. Often engineers and mathematicians function primarily out of the left brain.

We estimate that very few people work predominantly from the left brain, and that the vast majority respond to right brain communication. This explains why starting a sermon with abstract, left brain words like "justification by faith" will not register with most people. It also makes clear why beginning a sermon with George's 13,13,13 story rings the bell.

Furthermore, most left brain dominant people work in a left brain dominant environment: actuaries for insurance companies, computer programmers for software corporations, chemical researchers for pharmaceutical businesses, etc. But even when left brain people come to church, they normally think in right brain categories because of the different environment. Thus stories may

---

Left Brain Functions

- *Analysis*
- *Speech*
- *Language*
- *Math*
- *Logic*

---

well capture attention, whereas technical exegetical observations probably leave even the left-brainers dumbfounded.

We can, however, have too much right brain material. In that case we become pulpit entertainers rather than substantive gospel communicators. We dare not leave the story of 13,13,13 George as is. We must ask questions that probe the mind: What happened to George? How did religious experience alter his lifestyle? Did he experience what we call justification by faith?

Ah! At last we come to *justification by faith*, that difficult expression. But now we have the attention of our people and they will listen. They have an investment in the subject, the investment established because George's story paved the way for in-depth considerations. Even when we discuss justification by faith, we can sprinkle our comments with Martin Luther stories or courtroom scenes, and especially the gospel story of the cross to help our people comprehend what God has done for his children.

So we aim at building real Christians. We want strong disciples, people who construct their houses not on sand, but solid rock. To mix left and right brain materials appropriately helps build New Testament followers of Jesus Christ. But to overdo left brain content produces boredom. To employ too much right brain material results in skin-deep Christians. In the following story we see the inter-weaving of right and left brain material:

> Do we *really* believe that God *really* answers prayer? Years ago there was a small town in Kansas which prided itself on the fact there were no establishments that sold liquor in the town. Eventually, however, an enterprising fellow with a sharp eye for a fast buck came along and built a night club right on

the main street. The town was shocked. Members of the town's leading church became so upset over what they viewed as a sinful intrusion into the life of the community that they conducted all-night prayer vigils. They fervently prayed that God would somehow put an end to this "den of iniquity."

Amazingly enough, a short time later a bolt of lightning struck the night club. It was totally destroyed!

The night club owner was told that the church members had been praying for the destruction of his club. He sued the church and its members for damages. His attorney claimed that the prayers of the church had caused the loss of the club. The church's attorney, on the other hand, argued that the prayers of the church members had nothing whatever to do with the destruction of the club. Since lightning is legally considered to be an 'act of God,' the case was eventually thrown out of court.

But the judge, in writing his opinion, made a very pertinent remark. "It is the opinion of this court that wherever the blame lies for the fire, the night club owner apparently is the one who believes in prayer while the church members clearly do not."

(Told by Don Robertson in *Dear You*,
a Word Book publication.)

Now then, the genius of that illustration, in addition to the probing quality of it, lies in its co-mingling of left and right brain elements. Note the picture (right brain) material: night club, main street of a Kansas town, the church, the all night prayer meetings, lightning, the courtroom, the judge. The picture pattern, from beginning to end, holds the story together.

Now look at the left brain matter: Does God really answer prayer?—an abstract concern. What about prayer itself, sin, intercession, the arguments, an "act of God," a written opinion? Without the left brain dimension of the story, substance becomes thin. And just there lies the challenge of the preacher: colorful stories entertain but substance builds faith. Many Christians see no problem with prayer; thoughtful disciples know intercession comes with complex challenges.

In summary, our task as preachers lies not only in capturing attention with right brain stories, pictures and color, but also with probes to help our people process their faith.

We can benefit further from what psychologists call NLP, *Neurolinguistic Programming.* Behaviorists have learned that human beings process messages in one of three ways: by hearing, seeing, or handling. One of the three takes the dominant position in every human being. Some, then, learn primarily by hearing; for these people words and sounds carry significant meaning. Others comprehend fundamentally by seeing; these persons we call visual learners as we call hearing-dominant people auditory learners. Still other people receive information by a hands-on experience; we call these kinesthetic learners.

Visual people often use such language as, "I see what you mean"; auditory people may say, "I hear what you say";

NLP (Neurolinguistic Programming)
- *Auditory Dominance*
- *Visual Dominance*
- *Experiential Dominance (Kinesthetic)*

and kinesthetic learners need to *sense,* to get the feel of—as in hands-on experience—to grasp reality. Visual learners need to see to process information, so pictures on the screen of the mind facilitate learning. They need to *see,* to *watch* a picture unfold. Auditory learners like verbal directions and appreciate words. Kinesthetic learners need to *feel* their world. For example, they like to sense the excitement of a football game.

NLP tells the preacher he or she must relate to all three receiver types. Note the three types in the illustration of the club that burned by lightning. The visual material in the story looms vividly enough: lightning, people on their knees, the night club. The writer of the story weaves in the auditory dimension too: the sound of thunder, the voices of the people in prayer, the speech of the judge. And the kinesthetic or hands-on comes in for its share too: one can *feel* the "fast buck," *smell* the beer bottles, *sit* on the hard benches in the courtroom.

The Bible speaks to all three learning styles. For example, 1 John 1:1, "We declare to you what was from the beginning, what we have heard, what we have seen with our eyes, what we have looked at and touched with our hands, concerning the word of life."

We have looked at how to start a sermon, how to build the body with picture material, how to use pictures that appeal to all three learning dominances. Now we need to say a word about **concluding** the homily. Wrap up your presentation quickly, to the point, and with precision. You may wish to use a picture again, an illustration that puts in a nutshell the single truth you want your people to carry home with them. Or you can summarize, rehearsing the three major concerns of the sermon. Sometimes you can ask one or two, even three, crucial questions, measuring your pace, pausing, letting the implications of the message sink deeply into minds and hearts. Whatever method you choose to conclude, make clear the invitation of Christ to say "yes" to his offer of spiritual advance.

A pastor found himself with only eight minutes to preach. The worship period, overextended, left him no choice but to speak briefly. He addressed his congregation on loving one's enemies. He illustrated his sermon powerfully, then saw his time had gone. With slow pace and appropriate tonal emphasis, he concluded with one eloquent thrust: "Don't be anybody's enemy." The sanctuary, sober and completely silent, could not miss the preacher's heart cry.

Linguistics

We come next to the second technique, one that follows closely the technique called homiletics. We call this skill *linguistics*. Here we concern ourselves with language usage: word selection, syntax, grammar, economy—any of the factors that go into sculpting ideas in clear, comprehensible speech.

Precisionists communicate. No law of declamation supersedes this two word statement.

My mother loved making jello salads. On a Sunday after church, guests arrived to sit at our dinner table. Mom, in the kitchen, couldn't get the jello out of the tin mold. So she put warm water on the mold only to have the heat work too well. The jello collapsed. Mother worked desperately, trying to reassemble the green jello into its intended shape. When language does not take its proper shape, ideas collapse. Precise wording gives shape to the truths intended for communication.

How do we manage language so ideas take meaningful form? **Reading** the best literature provides models of good writing. Take, for example, Washington Irving. The descriptions in *The Legend of Sleepy Hollow* paint memorable scenes. Word choice and word sequence play their parts in the gripping portraits of Ichabod Crane, Brom, the farmer's daughter, and the other characters in the story. The landscape, the animals, the tea tables—all make indelible impressions on the minds of Irving's readers.

More recent writers, too, use words with precision. C. S. Lewis, J. R. R. Tolkien, and Thomas Merton stand out as examples. Today's Christian authors who model good English include Richard Foster, Henri Nouwen, and Dallas Willard. Secular magazines, too, can show us how to use language skillfully…secular periodicals like *Time*, *The New York Times*, and *The Washington Post*. Religious papers such as *Leadership*, *Christian History*, and *Christianity Today* demonstrate a fine level of editing.

Good writers relish their love affair with words. Filling our minds with the best English influences the tongue, nudging us to observe grammatical and linguistic standards. Observers of high linguistic standards speak clearly, understandably. Significantly, following standards carries moral implications too. To use sloppy English can give, for example, a kind of tacit permission to stretch the truth, to sound terribly good, and thus to violate accuracy. Preachers have made a name for themselves as exaggerators. Any misshaping of the truth does disservice to the church of Jesus Christ, whose name means integrity.

Good writers, like good preachers, check their facts. They do research, consult authorities, get help from librarians. One wonders how often worshippers, especially impressionable youth, have heard the preacher tell falsehoods as fact. One wonders further if carelessness does not give permission to youth and others to lie, cheat, and mislead. "If the preacher can say it, so can I." Precision makes its demands on God's servants. True, all human beings, including clergy, err. Our unswerving goal, however, is integrity.

A second way to develop into precisionists, relates to **writing.** We read good models of the language, then follow their example, never imitating another writer, but putting our unique selves into the composition of sermons. If one writes out his or her sermons consistently, oral delivery will come in more precise terms. No, one must not read from the manuscript in delivery, but the pen-to-paper preparation creates awareness of language and orients the preacher to the ideas for presentation.

Write out your sermons, word for word, in the first three years of ministry, and you will experience two grand rewards: (1) facility with the language in public (even when you must "say a few words" at the church potluck), and (2) you will find the discipline so workable and rewarding that you will reduce your sermons to written form for the rest of your ministry.

Now a word about the process of writing. First, have at hand basic reference tools: a good desk dictionary, an unabridged dictionary for occasional reference, a word finder, and a grammar and syntax tool. A good handy dictionary is *Merriam Webster's Collegiate Dictionary.* For an unabridged, you may want to get *Webster's New Twentieth Century Dictionary Unabridged* or *The Oxford English Dictionary* (the latter available in micro-print version). The best word finder is Rodale's *The Synonym Finder.* The new Strunk and White, *Elements of Style* continues its status as a grammar and syntax guide. Other useful reference tools you will find listed in "100 Books of the Preacher's Library" towards the close of this book.

We come now to a third way of developing into precisionists; namely, **listening.** Attentive and creative listening can enhance one's capacity with the English language. Find the most fluent and skillful conversationalists. Have coffee with them frequently. Every church has gifted communicators in membership. Also, observe the flow of language in a newscaster like Peter Jennings, and notice the word choice in a television personality such as D. James Kennedy, or the radio preacher, Charles Swindoll.

Sometimes, too, parishioners will correct the preacher's English. God graces every local congregation with at least one grammarian! The wise preacher evaluates critiques, learning from the good and ignoring the anger and ego-tripping of insecure people.

In sum, turning ourselves into precisionists, never child's play, demands focus on the handling of both language and ideas. God desires deeply to make us preachers worthy of the trust of our people.[3]

Tonetics

We come now to a third technique factor, *tonetics*, or tone. Find your vocal median. You may need to sit at the piano and sing up and down the scale until you find your natural and comfortable center. Then, move tonally up and down and around that center. Make your center home base. Public speakers often speak in higher than natural tones because we instinctively know people hear higher tones better than lower ones. The answer to audibility comes not from unnatural tonal level but in enunciation and projection.

• *Find your vocal median*

• *Project from the diaphragm*

• *Cultivate your voice to say "invitation"*

Projection power originates not so much from the thorax as the diaphragm. When tone comes primarily from the throat area, hoarseness can ensue and eventually nodules on the vocal chords, a disease yielding only to difficult treatment (surgery, drug therapy or long periods of silence). The diaphragm, a muscle in the abdominal part of the anatomy, is the source of power for vocal projection. Human beings sing and speak best by diaphragmatic projection. To correct bad habits, some public people

---

[3]On theories of language, see the article by John S. McClure, "Language, Theories of" in *Concise Encyclopedia of Preaching*, pp. 292ff.

must take voice lessons—a most worthwhile investment of time and money, since the speaking voice has so much to do with the perception of leadership qualities.

Some great preachers have worked on tonal quality throughout their lives. My friend, Bishop Donald Bastian, will go to the piano on a Saturday night before preaching Sunday morning, sing up and down the scales, vocalizing, orienting his voice for public speech. The bottom line: Cultivate your voice to say "invitation," making it heard, warm, and welcoming.

Kinesics

We look now at a fourth and final component of technique: *kinesics.* By this we refer to body language. Scientists tell us 60 to 80 percent of communication relates to physical projection. The way one stands, posture, the position of the legs, the use of hands and arms—all relate to clear or fuzzy presentation. Even the way one dresses says something good, bad or indifferent.

Excess body movement confuses listeners. Speakers communicate—inevitable as soon as one stands to his or her feet to talk in public—for the public preacher cannot escape communicating. What one says, in words, tone, and kinesics, spells either clarity or confusion.[4] To flail the air, to point in one direction and look in another, to walk back and forth—any such diverting body projection robs

- *Body language is 60 to 80% of our communication*

- *Beware of cognitive dissonance*

- *Eye contact is most important*

listeners of focus. The aim: say with your body what your lips articulate. To declare one thing with the body and another with the tongue creates what we call *cognitive dissonance.* Such disharmony sprays London fog on the psyches of hearers.

---

[4]See Charles L. Barlow, "Delivery of Sermons," in *Concise Encyclopedia of Preaching*, pp. 99ff, especially the carefully crafted paragraph on p. 101 beginning, "Pauses, no less …."

Eyes telegraph the most eloquent bodily communication known to human beings. To hold the eye of a parishioner, not too long but enough to make contact, assists greatly not only in getting through to the person with whom you locked eyes, but to those around that person. That law of public communication means the preacher can move from section to section of the sanctuary, letting people know the message relates to each person. Even if the preacher cannot see the eyes of people toward the back of the church or in the balcony, to look where people's eyes are leaves the sense of contact.

To preach well, one must organize material to suit the listening capacities of human beings. The technique called *homiletics* provides the framework for the organization of biblical matter. Related techniques include linguistics, tonetics, and kinesics.

2

William Barclay's Principles (Continued)

"In all speaking, especially in preaching, naturalness, genuineness, even though awkward, is really more effective for all the highest ends, than the most eloquent artificiality."
—John A. Broadus, in Richard Lischer, *Theories of Preaching,* p. 105

Preaching must be by compulsion.

Dr. Barclay's second principle says preaching must be by compulsion. The term *compulsion* comes from the Latin term meaning *force.* The preacher must sense a driving force that says, "I *must* preach the gospel."

Right on! A truly called minister of the gospel can hardly wait to preach the next sermon. The gospel burns in heart and soul; the spirit excites to homiletical possibilities; imagination ignites with illustrative possibilities.

Jeremiah *had* to prophesy. His depressive spirit could not prevent him announcing the judgment of God nor his offer of mercy. Who would want the words of the prophet omitted from the biblical canon?

Moses tried to dodge God's call to preach, insisting he had no oratorical gifts. God put him in a corner and asked if he didn't have a mouth. The Almighty would help him use that mouth. Finally God had to send Aaron to help Moses, but at last Moses caught fire. The book of Deuteronomy, actually a series of sermons, holds for all time Moses' convictions inspired by the living God.

Who can forget St. Paul? Not a likely candidate for a fiery preacher, but after Damascus Road and subsequent to his years in Arabia, Paul followed the command of Christ to preach. With great power he declared, "Woe is me if I preach not the Gospel!"

William Barclay caps the climax when he summarizes his second principle of preaching, *compulsion,* with these forceful sentences: "Preaching cannot be a spare time hobby or a pleasant sideline. The preacher is the man who speaks because he cannot keep silent." [1]

Preaching must be by conviction.

Principle three reads like this: preaching must be by conviction. Here we confront a law of communication: **Desperate conviction communicates**. In less dramatic language, the preacher who really means business gets through to the audience.

A corollary law says **strong belief communicates security**. A spirit of compromise will not communicate the surety of the gospel. Only a know-so faith does that. Strong Christian disciples result from Rock of Gibraltar preaching. Charles Spurgeon counseled his preachers to dive in the water, not put a toe in here and a hand in there. Dive in for all you're worth, he admonished. And that's precisely what the great nineteenth century English preacher did.

Barclay captures his third principle in a telling phrase, "the accent of conviction." That tone of certitude marks compelling pulpit speech; the preacher speaks with authority and convinces sinners of the need to repent, reminds nominal Christians of Jesus' require-

---

[1]Barclay, *Autobiography,* p. 76.

ment to leave all and follow him, and admonishes mature disciples to continue in the grand enterprise of spiritual formation.[2]

Preaching must come from experience.

William Barclay's fourth principle: Preaching must come from experience. By that he means one must know from personal encounter the Scripture preached. To preach "beyond" one's experience bars both speaker and audience from authenticity, yet Barclay admonishes us to preach the whole Bible.

At this point the preacher confronts a dilemma: How can one proclaim Scripture one has not experienced? Yet Barclay insists pastors deliberately preach from the entire Bible. He even chides pulpit people whose Bibles show, by thumb prints, which portions of Holy Writ one favors. We usually favor the Gospels, portions of the Epistles, certain Psalms, some of the Old

- *Preach the whole Scriptures.*
- *Deliberately wrestle with hidden Scriptures.*

Testament stories, etc. But what about the vast stretches of Scripture that go untouched, asks Professor Barclay.

Barclay's answer calls for facing the challenge of "experiencing" those portions of the Bible to which one may not naturally migrate. Every preacher has his or her own favorite passages; likewise, each preacher has his or her own "avoidance" Scriptures. Some find 2 Peter difficult to cope with; others would rather not deal with the book of Revelation; still others prefer not to handle a difficult book like Daniel.

One answer to the avoidance temptation lies in lectionary preaching, which we will consider a bit later. Another way to cover the full range of Scripture lies in a rather complete check sheet of

---

[2]Barclay says eloquently, "The listener will always know when a man believes intensely in what he says, and even if the listener does not agree, even if he thinks the speaker is misguided, he respects the accent of conviction."

doctrinal and moral truths. An example of such a check sheet begins on page 19.

The bottom line: Deliberately wrestle with unfamiliar portions of Scripture, thus *experiencing* in some measure the truth inherent in such passages. We all need help engaging in such an enterprise. Two suggestions: (1) Remind yourself that serious exegetical study of a passage, at first foreign to one, is indeed a form of *experience*. Our memory banks, chock full of memories, will find connection points with facets of truth in any passage. Pictures will come to mind to make clear God's Word, and those very illustrations will uncover once hidden meanings. (2) Recall a learning experience analogous to a fresh encounter with Scripture. How well I remember an invitation to dedicate an airplane. Such an assignment! I had experienced the dedication of churches and religious education buildings, but an airplane?

The story behind that still fascinates me. A seminarian with a pilot's license wanted to fly his professors to their weekend preaching assignments, especially places difficult to go to on commercial airlines. He dreamed of a landing field in Wilmore, the home of Asbury Theological Seminary. Bill even collected enough money to purchase a fine airplane, and now wanted it dedicated to the glory of God and his service.

My first task after saying yes to the invitation related to learning about airplanes. I had flown thousands of miles across our country and overseas, but I had never bothered to school myself in a plane's flight panel or its construction. Bill graciously took me to his plane at Blue Grass Field, Lexington; he showed me the cockpit, described the structure of the plane, and gave me first lessons in under-standing his flying machine. Once I had *experienced* the plane I could say something meaningful, at least at the elementary level. The service in the airport hanger proved a spiritually moving event.

No, one does not need to know *everything* about a passage to speak from it authentically. One does need to encounter the Scripture portion genuinely. That will require deliberate wrestling with the passage.

Subject Check Sheet

Adultery							
Angels							
Anthropology							
Ascension							
Assurance							
Atonement							
Authority							
Baptism							
Belief							
Blood							
Body of Christ							
Bondage							
Christian Life							
Christology							
Church							
Circumcision							
Communion							
Community							
Compassion							
Conscience							
Conversion							

Covenant							
Creation							
Cross							
Crucifixion							
Death							
Devil							
Divorce							
Dreams							
Election							
Eschatology							
Eternal Life							
Evil							
Faith							
The Fall							
Family							
Fasting							
Fear of God							
Fire							
Flesh							
Forgiveness							
Free Will							
Freedom							

Friendship							
God							
Grace							
Guilt							
Heart							
Heaven							
Holiness of God							
Holy Spirit							
Hope							
Idolatry							
Image of God							
Immortality							
Incarnation							
Intercession							
Joy							
Jublilee							
Justice							
Justification							
King							
Kingdom of God							
Law							
Legalism							

Love								
Love of God								
Lovingkindness of God								
Lying								
Man								
Marriage								
Mercy								
Messiah								
Ministry								
Miracles								
Morality, Sexual								
Mystery of the Kingdom								
Name								
Nature								
Neighbor, Love for								
New Life in Christ								
Oaths								
Obedience								
Omnipotence								
Optimism								
Pacifism								
Passover								

Patience							
Peace							
Pentecost							
People of God							
Person of Christ							
Power of God							
Power							
Prayer							
Predestination							
Priesthood							
Providence							
Repentance							
Responsibility							
Resurrection							
Righteousness of God							
Sabbath							
Sacrificial Worship							
Salvation							
Sanctification							
Scapegoat							
Simplicity							
Sin							

Son of God							
Son of Men							
Soul							
Sovereignty							
Spiritual Gifts							
Suffering							
Syncretism							
Tabernacle							
Temple							
Transcendence							
Trinity							
Trust							
Unity							
War							
Wisdom							
Women							
Word of God							
Work							
Works							
Worship							
Wrath of God							

Source unknown.

Preaching must be biblically and credally centered.

We come to principle five: preaching must be biblically and credally centered. Here we insist on expository preaching. We need also to remind ourselves that today we do exposition in many ways. The old verse by verse pattern does not work too well in our time, though now and again we hear a pulpit communicator who uses that method well. The essence of contemporary exposition lies in isolating truth from the pericope (the preaching passage) and translating it into stories and pictures that communicate to the living world of today. This large view of preaching opens the door to a thousand creative possibilities. Some of those we will describe and demonstrate in subsequent chapters of this book.

At this point, we must underscore the necessity of conveying Bible facts and truths to our people. Everyone knows the wretched level of biblical literacy in our time. This accounts for far more than ignorance of facts; it relates to lifestyle. The purpose of gospel preaching lies in discipling our people for consistent Christlike living.

The tradition of topical preaching does not enjoy a consistent track record of helping people live like Jesus. Moralistic essays, however well illustrated, will not do the job. Our secular culture conditions us to do "nice" sermons that make people feel good, but allow them to continue living in their sins. Authentic biblical preaching changes lives.

And why does Professor Barclay insist on adding *credally* to this fifth principle? The official creeds of the church provide us with one method of interpreting Scripture; they also help us organize the Bible into manageable chunks of truth.

Take, for example, the Apostles' Creed. It comes in three paragraphs, the first relating to the Father, the second to the Son, and the third to the Holy Spirit. Therein emerges a fine outline for a series of sermons on this most celebrated of creeds. More, every part of that classic credal statement relates intimately to Scripture. One would have a difficult time preaching the Creed apart from the Bible.

Let us also remind ourselves that our people desperately need to hear and repeat the Apostles' Creed, that doing so can anchor their beliefs in secure faith and authentic hope. To use the Creed often in public worship, then to preach from it, will assist our parishioners to strengthen trust and bring inspiration without which we cannot live freely, meaningfully, and joyously.

Preaching ought to be systematic.

Dr. Barclay reveals his pastor's heart when he tells us his sixth principle: preaching ought to be systematic. He longs to see church-goers get the full picture of biblical truth meaningfully sequenced, thus building step-by-step Christian character and knowledge.[3]

How do we preach systematically? Lectionary preaching defines one way. Two classic patterns have held sway historically: *lectio selecta* and *lectio continua*.

Take the latter first. *Lectio continua* relates to preaching through a book of the Bible. A college pastor did a long Sunday morning series on the book of Mark. He found himself saving time trying to decide what to preach Sunday by Sunday—"Why! I preach the next paragraph," he explained—and saddled—yes, that's the right term—with preaching passages he would really rather not handle. He learned a lot! He grappled with issues, and in the very struggle he, along with his people, identified sources of strength and victory.

One formidable challenge faces *lectio continua* exposition: some books, due to their length, can put off both preacher and people. One answer comes in selectivity, for example, in the book of Psalms. Why not preach a series from representative Psalms: 1, 19, 23, 46, etc? In this way, people will enjoy exposure to both the themes and rhythms of the Psalter, yet not suffer the boredom that often comes with too long a series of sermons. (How well I remember a young lady complaining about her pastor's over-long series on the Psalms!)

---

[3]Robert J. McCracken rightly says, "When biblical exposition is frequent and systematic it delivers a man from indulging his own predilections" (*The Making of the Sermon*, p. 31).

Yet sometimes our people want a very long succession of sermons on a single book. Zwingli, ushering in the Reformation in Zurich, Switzerland, preached weekdays at noon for something like three years through the book of Matthew. Matthew, a wise choice, is, according to some scholars, the first catechism of the early church. The first Gospel teaches the basic truths of biblical religion. Know that the people of Zurich experienced substantial orientation to the true gospel after Zwingli had finished the 28th chapter of Matthew.[4]

Meaningfully, the businessmen closed their shops at noon to come hear the Zurich reformer. When the Spirit of God moves on a people to listen consistently over a period of time to a book of the Bible—well, that signals a golden opportunity! This explains D. M. Lloyd-Jones' very long series of addresses from the book of Romans. He preached Sunday after Sunday, and for years, through that seminal Pauline book and produced volume after volume. For example, he devotes an entire tome (457 pages!) to Romans 8:17-39. (See *Romans: An Exposition of Chapter 8:17-39, The Final Perseverance of the Saints*. Grand Rapids: Zondervan, 1976.)

The more frequently employed lectionary scheme we call *lectio selecta*.[5] Many *selecta* programs exist: note the one in *The Book of Common Prayer*. Explore too, the eight denomination plan (regular scheme publications come in cycles; also commentaries to help the preacher prepare sermons) and the Roman Catholic arrangement. Many Lutheran groups also provide calendars. The list goes on. The purpose of *selecta* sermonizing comes through loud and clear: the systematic teaching of our people, covering the specific truths, as well as the grand sweep, of Christian doctrine.

Barclay complains that any pulpit Bible shows, by thumb prints (that again!), preaching from favorite passages, but leaves great

---

[4]See G. R. Potter, *Zwingli*, p. 60. See also Andrew W. Blackwood's *Preaching from Samuel*, an attempt to help the preacher go through an entire book (Blackwood takes 1 and 2 Samuel as one book).

[5]J. J. von Allman argues against anything like an enforced ecumenical lectionary because Christianity's theologies are not truly unified. See his *Preaching and Congregation*, p. 46.

stretches of Scripture untouched. If preachers do not wish always to preach from a prepared lectionary, or work through a book of the Bible, they can check passages and subjects against a systematic theology book (simply place check marks alongside topics in the table of contents), to guarantee no omissions. A friend awakened to an omission in his preaching: the ascension of our Lord. He got busy and prepared a sermon on the subject.

Filing preaching plans and examining them yearly, every three years, and each five years, will put the sweep of one's preaching into perspective. My friend Henry does that. He blocks out a schedule of Sundays on ordinary typing paper and tapes four or five sheets together to accommodate the church year. He writes in the special Sundays (Mothers' Day, Easter, etc.), notes the services at which he will not preach (a Sunday evening film, e.g.), then produces his own *lectio selecta*. Over the years, he makes sure he covers the full spectrum of biblical truth. To my knowledge, Henry has never lost a parishioner to a cult. (Cults thrive on neglected truth areas–e.g., Christian Science emerged as a result of the neglect of teaching about healing in the church.)

Preaching ought to be teaching.

Now comes Professor Barclay's seventh principle: preaching ought to be teaching. And thereby hangs a pattern of homiletical truth we must analyze.

Barclay reminds us of four salient terms for preaching: **Kerygma**, **Didache**, **Paraklesis**, and **Homilia**. We need to define these four terms. *Kerygma* relates to the non-negotiable truths of the saving gospel. Robert Mounce charts the *Kerygma* as follows:

A proclamation of the

1. Death,
2. Resurrection, and
3. Exaltation of our Lord,
4. All seen as the fulfillment of prophecy and
5. Involving man's responsibility.

The resultant evaluation of Jesus as both

6. Lord and
7. Christ.

On this basis hearers of the gospel must

8. Repent and
9. Receive forgiveness of sins.[6]

This outline of the gospel points to the message that saves. Every sermon, to be a gospel sermon, must have some element or elements of the *Kerygma* in it. Hopefully, every sermon will indeed embrace *Kerygma*, for that very content God uses to bring his people to repentance and therefore personal salvation.

Didache, intimately associated with *Kerygma*, relates to the explanation of the *Kerygma* in terms of application. One must repent, for example, but upon repentance, how does behavior change? In other words, the ethical implications of being a Christian come to light in didactic preaching. What one believes comes into play in *Kerygma*; *how* one lives out that belief comes into play in *Didache*.[7]

Paraklesis we define as exhortation or encouragement. The New Testament sees exhortation not as scolding but encouragement. Every sermon must articulate reassurance and strong faith. God calls the preacher to inspire the people. They need buoying, nerving for the new week, which may involve visiting the doctor under difficult circumstances, wrestling through divorce proceedings, going to court with a son or daughter, or just living victoriously through ordinary days. Preachers make up a significant part of the

---

[6]For further help and instruction, see Robert H. Mounce, *The Essential Nature of New Testament Preaching* and John R. W. Stott, *The Preacher's Portrait*.

[7]"We have learned to make a distinction between 'Kerygma' and 'didache' (=teaching), but 'didache,' which is not pervaded by the life breath of 'kerygma,' is not a really authentic communication of the Christian message" (Hendrick Kraemer, *Communication of the Christian Faith*, p. 24). For a further analysis of *Kerygma* and *Didache*, see Donald E. Demaray, *Introduction to Homiletics*, pp. 36–39.

booster community. They are God's cheerleaders, bringing hope firmly rooted in the Word of God. *Paraklesis* constitutes a most important function of the preaching ministry.

Homilia, the fourth term for preaching, opens the door to addressing any subject appropriate for the pulpit. Every preacher exercises freedom to talk about relevant and immediate concerns.

When a horrible train accident occurred, ambulances sounded their sirens for hours. Paramedics, swamped by the carnage, worked into the night. Hospitals struggled with overcrowding. At such time, local pastors might well talk to their people about the comforting mercies of medical professionals, the presence of the Lord in tragedy, or divine healing power. Any of those subjects could serve to strengthen a community in time of tragedy, even though the planned preaching passage announced weeks in advance did not come to expected fruition.

- **Kergma:**
  the non-negotiable
- **Didache:**
  the instruction
- **Paraklesis:**
  exhortation/ encouragement
- **Homilia:**
  any subject in light of Christian truth

Now then, we need to ask which of these four preaching words depict our most important task. No one doubts *Kerygma* must find a place in every gospel sermon. Nor do we question the need for encouragement, *paraklesis*. Still further, we could never avoid *homilia*, for one must stay sensitive to altering the preaching program when needed. But of the four kinds of preaching, William Barclay declares the most needed in our western culture has to do with *Didache*, teaching. Our people must learn the Bible and absorb its ethical implications for Christian living. When we teach the Bible our people can advance in spiritual formation and move into serious discipleship. The bottom line: *Every sermon must teach.* Come to

think about it, who likes to hear a message that brings to the ear no
new ideas? Interest grows with information.[8]

The preacher must be a continuing learner.

We come now to principle number eight: The preacher must be a
continuing learner. Herein we confront two laws: The first, **giving
out requires taking in.** Preachers cannot continually contribute to
others unless they refurbish mind and spirit; otherwise, they burn
out very quickly.

The second law is this: **the excited learner communicates.**
Enthusiasm generates listenability, which in turn promotes the integration of truth. Dullards do not communicate successfully.
Inspired speakers invest time in preparation and that shows in the
excited delivery of truth. And herein lies a secret of gospel
communication: The more one lives with a passage, finding pictures
to illustrate it, observing its nuances, translating it into
contemporary communicable forms—i.e., the more one absorbs
him or herself in the preaching pericope—the greater the
enthusiasm at the moment of pulpit delivery.

Now we come to a crucial question about preparation. How does
one prepare with the absorbed involvement that leads to
enthusiastic sermon delivery? Four procedures may help.

(1) *Study on a clean desk.* A difficult assignment, to be sure, for
we all wrestle with finding the tops of our desks. Clutter,
assignments, notes to return phone messages—all these and more
inundate us.

One answer lies in having two work stations, one for the flow of
administrative labor and the other for sermon study. Another
answer lies not in having a physically clear desk, but in clearing the
mind of to-do items, thus freeing the preacher to engage in simple

---

[8]Roland Bainton shows the relation of teaching and preaching, and their balance in
Luther's ministry: "As Luther's sermons were often didactic, so were his lectures
commonly sermonic. He was always teaching, whether in the classroom or the pulpit;
and he was always preaching, whether in the pulpit or in the classroom" (*Here I Stand*,
p. 355).

and direct thinking. Whatever one's solution, the careful sermon preparer wants to come to the task with openness and excitement.

(2) A second step in absorbed preparation relates to the very paper on which one makes notes. *Start with a clean sheet*, for example a legal pad. The sight of empty paper suggests clearing the mind, readying it for serious engagement with the text.

(3) A third step: *work with pen poised to record anything at all.* The most amazing observations and thoughts come to one when making preliminary notes for a sermon. Do not expect to use all you record, but do not be surprised if you verbalize items in sermon delivery you did not expect to employ, yet noted on early work sheets. Emptying the mind of all that occurs to it about the text yields rich fruit and eventually assists in shaping a homiletical structure that communicates the truth at hand with power.

(4) *Now commit yourself, in these beginning stages of preparation, to an uninterrupted two hour block of time.* In my teaching of preaching, I used to tell students and preachers at conferences to invest an hour of preparation for every minute of delivery. So a twenty-minute sermon would take twenty hours of preparation. That classic pattern, impractical in our busy world, rarely works today. I have, in recent years, instructed people to work early in the week in a two hour block. Usually that much time will yield a sermon structure—an outline, a flow chart, a narrative framework, whatever—and during the rest of the week current ideas and relevant pictures to enrich the fledgling structure will come to one's mind. Then one can put the whole into script towards the end of the week; after that, reduce the manuscript to simple outline.

The principle involved here relates to processing an idea, watching it develop and bringing it to presentable form. But a real pastoral issue confronts busy ministers: How do I find even two uninterrupted hours? Each year I do preaching conferences for Salvation Army officers. They typify clergy in the extreme busyness of their weekly endeavors. Social work, thrift shops, hospital visitation, civic duties, and all the rest make finding two hours of uninterrupted time a challenge. Actually, the Salvationist officers only represent what all clergy struggle with: time, quality time, for sermon preparation.

The answer lies in priorities. If the preacher really believes in a theology of preaching that says God uses the proclaimed word as his *chief* means of saving the lost and developing disciples, then he or she will put sermon preparation in its proper place (1 Cor. 1:21, Gal. 1:16; Acts 9:20). With that philosophy fixed, he or she will make a habit of setting aside time. I have a friend who put a sign on his study door at the church at certain times of the week: PLEASE DO NOT DISTURB. SERMON UNDER CONSTRUCTION. Everyone in that parish knew the pastor meant business, and when he rose to preach twice each Sunday, they heard something eminently worthwhile. He refused to allow interruption except for emergencies.

How to continue learning? Invest yourself in preparation.

Preaching must be intelligible.

That brings us to the ninth of Barclay's principles: preaching must be intelligible.[9] How do we become intelligible? By recognizing three things, says Barclay: (1) People *hear* sermons; (2) Preachers live in their *own world*; (3) Only preachers must communicate to *everyone*.

First, our people *hear* sermons. No playbacks, as on TV sports casts. I love tennis. When I watch a tennis match on television, each play comes back on the screen from at least two vantage points, sometimes three, and often we see the repeat of the play as first telecast. Preachers have no such options. They must use creative repetition, engaging phrases, memorable structures—anything and everything to make their material easy to remember.

---

[9]Sir Mounstuart E. Grant Duff, referring to Frederick Denison Maurice, says candidly: "I went, as usual, to hear F. D. Maurice preach at Lincoln's Inn. I suppose I must have heard him, first and last, some thirty or forty times, and never carried away one clear idea or even the faintest conception of what he himself meant."

In this technological age, we must work diligently to make *heard* pulpit address communicative. In one way this challenge has its enormous benefits; people see as well as *hear* the preacher. The total preacher communicates in person.

So we need to remind ourselves to help our people listen. They welcome fresh information interestingly pictured. We also must remember that better than thirteen percent of our population suffers from hearing loss to some degree. To enunciate carefully, pronouncing vowels, articulating final D's and T's, sustaining -ing's—honoring every nuance of clear speech—contributes significantly to listenability.

Second, Barclay calls on preachers to remember they *live in their own world*. We read theology, listen to models of good preaching, live in the Scripture. But our people come from the plumber's shop, the carpenter's bench, the teacher's schoolroom, their minds filled with their worlds. One way to orient our people to the sacred message at hand is to start where they live.

A real life illustration, right out of contemporary society, may well ring the bell. Sometimes a slice of humor that lets the people know the preacher stays in touch with reality does the trick. We must make *contact*. Once made, we can translate ancient truth into living and contemporary categories.

Seminarians and young pastors just out of theological training often have a difficult time relating to people in their worlds. Minds full of systematic theology textbooks, exegesis papers, and historical data can bring a foreign mindset to the pulpit. Professor Barclay, who served many years as a theology professor at Glasgow University in Scotland, knew the very real need of relating meaningfully to people. He learned this first in his many years in the pastorate, then maintained this stance as a weekend preacher while teaching. At the height of his career, some say, ordinary people heralded him as the most popular preacher in Scotland.

Now then, to Barclay's third orientation concern: Only preachers must communicate to *everyone*. Specialists in medicine read papers to their colleagues; insurance brokers speak their own lingo;

scientists relate to people in their communities. But God assigns us preachers to talk understandably to medical specialists, insurance people, scientists, and everyone else.

A dentist asked his pastor for a book on theology. "I want to understand what you say on Sunday," he pleaded. His minister gave him a simple treatise, only to have him return the next week with the comment, "You preachers have your own vocabulary, don't you?"

John Wesley instructed his preachers to use "great plainness of speech," and suggested they read 1 John as a model of clear, simple language. We cannot get too simple. By that we do not mean *simplistic;* we do ourselves and the gospel no favor by preaching down to people. But we dare not use the specialized language of the theological academy without definition and explanation; nor can we afford to speak pedantically, forcing the scholarly world into the church. People must feel they belong, that they relate to the preacher and the message presented.

In summary of principle nine: intelligible preaching gets through and becomes the instrument of changed and enriched lives.

Preaching must be relevant, otherwise people won't come to hear us.

Principle ten of Barclay's eleven is that preaching must be relevant, otherwise people won't come to hear us. He talks about the "granite" faces in church, the unresponsive, those who wear a bored look. How do we change granite faces into warm respondents?

Barclay first suggests getting personal so people say, "That means me." Barclay did not mean, of course, to become so specific in relating to people that the preacher makes someone in the audience feel self-conscious. But to refer to the professions represented in the congregation: law, teaching, medicine—and to the vocations: maintenance, accounting, manufacture—with such references people feel recognized and identify with the message. They say, "I liked that sermon because I found myself in it."

People need also to sense the church speaks to their deepest needs. The way the pastor talks of grieving, of marriage and divorce, of single parents—when people see themselves vitally related to the church of Jesus Christ, the church becomes personal to them.

Some church people feel especially related when asked to participate in the worship and work of the church. Sunday School teachers, committee workers, lay people reading Scripture, Scout leaders participating with their scouts in a service specially designed for them, on occasion a lay speaker delivering the

- *Be personal.*

- *Demonstrate integrity.*

- *Make the Bible relevant.*

- *Use simple language.*

sermon—this, too, can help people say, "This is *my* church." Beyond the worship services, cooks and janitors and financiers can assist in the maintenance of the church and its programs, and help it advance the cause of Christ in the community. This also makes them feel the church belongs to them and they to the people of God.

Barclay tells us further that when the minister and the people live out their moral convictions, the world takes notice. When I think of this very relevant and significant fact, I recall the man who built my house. He had had a year of seminary, but later felt God calling him not into the professional ministry of the church, but the ministry of construction. He put his best into the houses he built: the finest lumber, careful workmanship, beautiful architecture. When the loan man came to examine our house as it neared completion, I found him staring into a corner of the living room. "What are you doing?" I asked. "I haven't seen mitering like this in a very long time," he replied. "I just looked under the house at the foundation and also examined the overall construction; this place will last until the Lord comes." Well, you can believe I felt good about my house and especially appreciative of the builder.

That kind of conscientiousness spells integrity, exactly what the world looks for and what church members want to see in their ministers and fellow church people. That's about as relevant as Christians can get!

Dr. Barclay goes on to encourage preachers to speak relevantly by announcing (and remember he was a New Testament professor), "Anything that makes the New Testament sound other than contemporary mistranslates it."[10] The New Testament, couched in *koine* (common, marketplace) Greek, God designed to communicate to ordinary people. When the 1611 King James Version appeared, it spoke in the everyday language of early seventeenth century England. Today Eugene Peterson's *Message* speaks to truck drivers, shopkeepers, daily laborers, and to us all. *The New Living Bible* uses very simple language, current, and immediately understood. We see at once why Barclay tells us to stay true to the spirit of the *koine* New Testament.

There is one thing without which all preaching is ineffective, and this is sincerity, sheer honesty.

Finally, we come to William Barclay's eleventh principle of preaching: there is one thing without which all preaching is ineffective, and this is sincerity, sheer honesty. Styles may differ and accents will come in patterns determined by where we grow up and the conditioning that inevitably accompanies early childhood. Dress will differ too. Patterns of worship come in all sorts of designs. People will tolerate differences, but the one factor people will not put up with is *insincerity*.

Bert E. Bradley observes the powerful role of sincerity in public address. He quotes psychologist Norman H. Anderson whose research shows that sincerity proved the one quality in a speaker (out of 555 options) people desired above all others.[11]

An old legend says the word sincerity comes from two Latin words, *cine cera*, without wax. The story goes that in the ancient world smart homemakers always held a ceramic pot to the sunlight

---

[10]*Autobiography*, p. 90.
[11]Bert E. Bradley, *Fundamentals of Speech Communication*, pp. 206-210.

to test it for cracks. Dishonest merchants covered breaks with wax. A sincere person, one "without cracks," comes across as authentic, as honest, a person of integrity.

Well, that old story does not hold much credence with today's philologists, but it speaks eloquently to what people want in their preachers. Interestingly, one does not have to announce himself or herself as sincere; that quality comes across as self-evident and reveals itself without the least trace of self-consciousness in the speaker.

Wherein lies the secret of sincerity? The New Testament answer says the touch of God's Spirit. The Spirit of Jesus cannot lie; his Spirit is the Spirit of truth. The preacher himself or herself is a sermon made so by the presence of God.

This explains why before every sermon the preacher must ask for fresh anointing, the grand secret of gospel truth communicated. God talks through the preacher who willingly becomes vulnerable and usable in the hand of Almighty God.

3

Interpretation: How to Determine Meanings

"The object of all preaching is to unlock meanings."
—Augustine, *De Doctrina Christiana*, IV. 5.7.

Interpretation is an art, a twofold art: discovery and communication. The biblical interpreter works by responsible guidelines,[1] making authentic discoveries of what texts actually say, then sharing those discoveries in language ordinary people can understand. The challenge presented to the preacher calls for establishing and following guidelines that make possible fruitful discoveries and therefore beneficial pulpit presentations.[2] No one assumes this an easy task.[3] Scripture interpretation is a skill which every serious preacher of the gospel gradually acquires. The interpreter's task requires time and experience to develop. Furthermore, interpretation, a spiritual and theological endeavor,

---

[1] John R. W. Stott, referring to James Barr's book, *Fundamentalism*, admits flatly, "We evangelicals have always been much better at defending the authority of the Bible than at wrestling with its interpretation" ("Are Evangelicals Fundamentalists?" *Christianity Today*, 8 September 1978, p. 45). For a set of representative perspectives on interpretation, see Richard Lischer, *Theories of Preaching: Selected Readings in the Homiletical Traditions* (Durham, NC: Labyrinth, 1987), Section IV.

[2] One of the best sets of guidelines is Robert A. Traina's *Methodical Bible Study*. Note also the articles on biblical interpretation (by Bernard Ramm, *et al.*) in Ralph G. Turnbull's *Baker's Dictionary of Practical Theology*, pp. 99-147.

[3] Donald C. Miller avers that "unless preaching involves a serious wrestling with biblical truth, it is not preaching at all" (*The Way to Biblical Preaching*, p. 28).

relates to our knowledge of God, and that too needs time to grow, as does our perception of what Scripture actually is.

Elementary Principles of Interpretation

1. Come to the passage as if you had never seen it.

Squarely face the fact that conditioning by the church in western culture makes this difficult. The very facing of that fact paves the way for seeing Scripture in fresh light.

Approach the Bible with new eyes. Do you remember what the world looked like when you stepped out of the eye doctor's office with brand new glasses? Suddenly you wondered if you had ever really seen the world. It came alive!

Give your selected preaching passage permission to make its own impression on you.[4] You do this whenever encountering anything new, as in traveling. Imagine visiting one of England's medieval cathedrals. Its immediate impact strikes you with great force. You cannot possibly comprehend, all at once, what you behold. However, after two or three hours the great structure begins to speak in clear, specific tones. When you return another day, you discover the cathedral prepared to give you more messages.

2. Take pencil in hand and record the most obvious facts about the passage.

Do not aim at much detail just now. Rather, simply record the most easily recognized data.

---

[4]Peter Stuhlmacher, in an article that cuts across much subjective hermeneutical practice and theory today, quotes the contemporary scholar Paul Ricoeur, who believes that to comprehend a text is "to understand oneself in the light of the text. It does not mean imposing upon the text one's own limited capacity for comprehension, but exposing oneself to the text…. It is not the [understanding] subject who forms… understanding, but…the self is formed by the 'subject matter' of the text." The Ricoeur quotation is from a lecture at Tübingen given in the mid-1970's. Stuhlmacher goes on to show that the earlier scholar, Adolf Schlatter, believed in the same kind of openness to the text. Schlatter even referred to the "misery" of Scripture when it cut painfully into one's consciousness ("Adolf Schlatter's Interpretation of Scripture," *New Testament Studies*, July 1978, pp. 433-34).

Looking at the exterior of the cathedral, you notice at once its enormous size, also the broad outline of its architecture. Inside, you see quickly the magic of repeated arches down the breathtaking nave, the play of light and shadow, of color and space, of statues and tombs. Then you move to the altars, the chapels, the hand-carved choir loft. After a bit, you have a broad outline of the structure and furnishings of the cathedral.

Just so in understanding a piece of Scripture. The cathedral spoke when you gave it a chance; Scripture speaks when you give it an open ear. For example, if you plan to preach from the book of Judges, you see the grand architectural design of the book very quickly: when the people keep God's laws, they thrive; when they live against those laws, they get into trouble. Light and shadow, insight and ignorance, worship good and false—all come into vivid and clear view.

3. Dig deeper.

General impressions of the Scripture passage have now made their mark on your mind—beginning impressions, of course, and subject to modification and enlargement. Foster that modification and enlargement by recording specific facts you see. List persons, places, times, events, teachings. Note what people do, how they act and react. Indicate teachings in the detail provided by Scripture (avoiding extensions of thought not actually in the passage). Observe the questions and declarations in the text.[5]

Developing a worksheet deepens comprehension of the passage under consideration. The pericope naturally determines the specific structure of the sheet.

The text of Matthew 8:5-13 in the New Revised Standard Version, marked by clarity and simplicity, reads as follows:

---

[5]Mortimer Adler's ideas about how to read help the interpreter-at-work. For example, "You should mark a book, underscore passages, go back and forth, raise all sorts of questions." Again, "The amount of intellectual activity that we put into reading a book is a measure of how well we are reading it" ("Conversation with an Author," *Book Digest*, May 1978, p. 241).

WORKSHEET
Matthew 8:5-13

WORKING TITLE: "The Healing of the Centurion's Servant"

PERSONS: Jesus   Abraham
                    centurion   Isaac
                    servant   Jacob
                    slave   "heirs of the kingdom"
                    soldiers

DIALOGUE: Centurion's request; Jesus' response
                    Centurion's further request with rationale
                    Jesus' amazed response to the group
                    Jesus' assurance of healing

TEACHINGS: The availability of Jesus
                    Faith works when exercised with authority
                    Jesus heals
                    Faith, healing, and authority all interrelated
                    The kingdom
                    Judgment

MOOD: Characterized by:
                    desperate need, appeal, and eagerness
                    authority
                    unworthiness
                    wonder
                    faith
                    belief
                    optimism
                    astonishment
                    kingdom of heaven

[5]When he entered Capernaum, a centurion came to him, appealing to him [6]and saying, "Lord, my servant is lying at home paralyzed, in terrible distress." [7]And he said to him, "I will come and cure him." [8]The centurion answered, "Lord, I am not worthy to have you come under my roof; but only speak the word, and my servant will be healed. [9]For I also am a man under authority, with soldiers under me; and I say to one, 'Go,' and he goes, and to another 'Come,' and he comes, and to my slave, 'Do this,' and the slave does it.' [10]When Jesus heard him, he was amazed and said to those who followed him, "Truly I tell you, in no one in Israel have I found such faith. [11]I tell you, many will come from east and west and will eat with Abraham and Isaac and Jacob in the kingdom of heaven, [12]while the heirs of the kingdom will be thrown into the outer darkness, where there will be weeping and gnashing of teeth." [13]And to the centurion Jesus said, "Go; let it be done for you according to your faith." And the servant was healed in that hour.

Clearly, producing a worksheet on such a passage is in itself part of the process of absorbing its meaning.

Now add to the worksheet; let it grow as you dig still deeper. You can, for example, become more detailed by:

1. Recording declarations verbatim.

2. Showing the flow of the material (Jesus enters Capernaum; centurion comes forward; etc.).

3. Indicating unexpected turns (a centurion appears to "tell" Jesus what to do).

4. Identifying persons (e.g., a centurion = an officer over 100 men).

The inquiring mind will find enough factors to keep fruitfully occupied for quite some time.[6]

---

[6]C. John Goldingway admonishes, "Keep listening to what the text says, hearing it through on the questions it raises (rather than cutting it off in mid-sentence because it has answered the questions we are interested in" ("Expounding the New Testament," *New Testament Interpretation*, ed. I. Howard Marshall, p. 361).

4. Identify the literary genre of the passage from which you prepare your sermon.

Ask: Do I work here with parable, history, poetry? What, specifically?

History, such as the Acts of the Apostles, we treat differently than apocalypse, such as the book of Revelation. Factual matter and dream literature call for their own methods of explanation. Both literary genres communicate truth: in the first instance, the acts of the Holy Spirit through chosen instruments; in the second, inspiration in visions and hidden language to a persecuted people. Historical overtones we do indeed find in Revelation, but *apocalypse* names the literary type. Grand moments of inspiration come in the Acts, but *history* identifies the literature. Accepting a piece of writing on its own terms assists in defining its intent, showing what it does, and creating a database from which to operate.

Suppose you work with Hebrew poetry. You could expect to encounter figures of speech, examples from history, and inspirational flow (the flow of Hebrew poetry, like a bird in flight, mounts ever higher and higher). The figures of speech may take the form of metaphor: "Be a rock of refuge for me, a strong fortress to save me!" (Ps. 31:2b). Or the figures can assume a simile configuration: "Your righteousness is like the mighty mountains" (Ps. 36:6a). Moreover, historical indicators appear frequently: "Remember the wonderful works he has done, his miracles, and the judgments he uttered" (Ps. 105:5). The rising tide of inspiration may take expression like this: "As for mortals, their days are like grass; they flourish like a flower of the field; for the wind passes over it, and it is gone, and its place knows it no more. But the steadfast love of the Lord is from everlasting to everlasting on those who fear him, and his righteousness to children's children, to those who keep his covenant and remember to do his commandments" (Ps. 103:15-18).

What about passages of mixed genre? How do we handle them? Take, for example, Isaiah 7:14: "Therefore the Lord himself will give you a sign. Look, the young woman is with child and shall bear a son, and shall name him Immanuel." Historically, Christians have taken this as prophecy, a specific type of literature; Jews tend to see the verse historically. Who wins the debate? Do both Christians and Jews stand correct? Do we in fact work with a double-genre passage, history and prophecy? Wrestle until you come up with an answer fully satisfying to yourself.[7]

5. Now find parallel or similar passages.

One of the rules of our trade declares, "Scripture interprets Scripture."[8] If you treat a passage in the synoptics, consult a good harmony of the Gospels to show parallel passages side by side.[9] If you aim to preach on 1 Corinthians 13, consult 1 John, where *love* appears about fifty times. If you wish to preach from Galatians 5:16-24, the paragraph contrasting the fruit of the flesh against the fruit of the Spirit, consult passages that throw light on the passage. The *Holman Study Bible* lists these cross-references: Mark 7:21; John 15:2; Rom. 1:28; 6:6, 12, 14; 7:15, 23; 8:14; 1 Cor. 6:9-10; Col. 3:15; James 3:17; Rev. 22:15.

Rich fruitage can come from studying passages with obvious commonalties, which at the same time enrich perspective. Take, for example, three accounts of blind men made to see: Matthew 9:27-31; John 9; Acts 9:1-9. A useful worksheet could include:

Teachings

Relational Concerns

    a. Who experienced healing?

    b. Who did the healing?

    c. Who reacted?

Cross-References

---

[7]Leland Ryken's book, *The Literature of the Bible*, may help you do the wrestling. He writes not as a critical biblical scholar but as a littérateur. Peter Rhea Jones, both a literature scholar and an exegete, may help too. See his article, "Biblical Hermeneutics," in the *Review and Expositor* for the spring of 1975.

[8]Luther put it this way: *Scriptura sui ipsius interpres.* ("Scripture is its own interpreter.") See John W. Doberstein, ed., *Minister's Prayer Book*, p. 379.

[9]See, e.g. the classic harmony: *Gospel Parallels: A Synopsis of the First Three Gospels*, the Huck-Lietzmann arrangement (New York: Nelson, 1949).

Contextual Concerns

Show both similarities and dissimilarities. Fill in your worksheet as study progresses (cf. the Matthew 8:5-13 worksheet on page 42).

6. Determine the context of the passage.

For healthy interpretation of a text one must attempt to define context, for "a text without its context is pretext."[10] What kinds of contextual challenges can we expect?

a. First, consider the larger context. Work with paragraphs, not isolated texts. Yes, a single verse may serve as a point of focus, but never as the kind of "proof texting" that forces unintended meanings. Get hold of the whole literary unit, allowing it to speak for itself.

Awareness of larger units—a chapter or even chapters—can yield a more complete conception of the pericope's meaning. The preacher can enrich understanding of a verse or a paragraph's intent also by examination of an outline of the whole book from which one's preaching portion comes.

Get a clear grasp of the overall thrust of the book's message. "The righteousness of God" is the grand theme of the book of Romans. That underlying communiqué of necessity will have a bearing on what you say about any paragraph within the book.

Still further, cognizance of the entire Bible keeps interpretation in line. The Bible's twofold theme, running like parallel scarlet threads throughout, is man's sin and God's remedy. Ultimately preachers will address this theme, in one way or another, whatever book of the

---

[10]The danger in using an alphabetically arranged guide to scriptural subjects, for example, Algerton C. P. Coote's *The Preacher's Homiletic Helper* is "proof texting"– making a verse or two say something not intended by the inspired writer. Really, the preacher using Coote allows the compiler of topics and verses to determine meanings. James Black puts the issue in perspective when he says, "In using a text, be sure that it is not really a concealed passage. In other words, it may not explain itself without its relevant context" (*The Mystery of Preaching*, p.143; cf. James W. Cox, *A Guide to Biblical Preaching*, p. 36). See also Robert Traina's *Methodical Bible Study.*

Bible texts come from, and whatever literary unit within a book one aims to interpret.

b. Next, one may single out the key words in the literary unit under study. Let them speak to you within the context of the surrounding words and their roles in the flow of language. You may need to consult wordbooks, lexicons, and dictionaries. But do your best to comprehend their specific meanings in the setting in which you find them.

A word takes on different meanings depending on the company it keeps. Take the word *love* as used in our everyday English. When your wife says, "I love that hat," or your husband, "I love that new car," the term has a very different meaning than it did on the night of your engagement when you announced, "I love you." Still another meaning comes into view when we talk about "brotherly love." Clearly, the context determines the meaning. *Love* carries many intentions.

Fortunately, modern wordbooks provide guides to contextual meanings, not only in the Scriptures but in ancient non-canonical literature as well. With this kind of help, also found in many commentaries today, we have much assistance in determining the precise meaning a word has in its context.

c. Then consider the context of time, place, and culture. The Bible, an ancient work of literature, calls us to discover historical information—knowledge of the cultural milieu, i.e.—for its interpretation. We cannot go back in time and stand where the biblical figures stood, but we do have three significant tools at our disposal for reconstructing the past.

(1) We can travel to Bible lands. We live in a most fortunate age; tours, with competent guides, travel to the Holy Land. Ministers should go as early in life as possible. Do make a Bible lands trip a priority. Once one has seen personally where Jesus and Paul lived and walked, one visualizes Scripture settings to enrich preaching. Lake Galilee comes alive, as do the other places our Lord visited!

(2) We can learn from those who have gone to the Bible lands. Travel documentaries and travelogue programs are especially

recommended. With screen and script, a specialist can make the Bible and its customs come alive. And do watch "Mysteries of the Bible" on Arts & Entertainment cable TV. Then, too, most Bible scholars in seminaries and colleges have gone to Bible lands to enrich their knowledge. Take advantage of continuing education opportunities.

(3) Finally, consult today's illustrated texts. Magnificent volumes in full color create interest and recreate settings. The purpose of all such study is, of course, to allow "the original impact of the text to happen again."[11]

Contexts of custom, geography, politics, and more all relate to the three discussed above. Contextual types necessary for study vary according to the book or passage under consideration. A good commentary provides at least introductory information about relevant contexts. You will find the *IVP Bible Background Commentary* (see Walton/Matthews, and Keener in the bibliography) especially useful, with its cultural background data on scriptural texts.

7. Determine the light which the passage throws on Christ.

The Bible reveals Christ. That truth must function as a working principle of all sound interpretation of Scripture. In Jesus the Christian finds the unity of Scripture. Because Jesus Christ defines the essence of our faith, true preaching must enrich knowledge of him.[12] The life of Christ as recorded in the Gospels interprets the rest of the Bible. Thus, we preach from the Acts, the Epistles, the

---

[11]Peter Rhea Jones uses this telling expression and adds, "The great expository preachers like Chrysostom, Spurgeon, and Thielicke have without exception sensed the hermeneutical issue and resolved it by being at home in the biblical world and their own era" ("Biblical Hermeneutics," p. 139).

[12]We must exercise caution, however, not to "read into" passages what isn't really there. The allegorists did this: Origen, Gregory of Nyssa, etc. (For a discussion of Gregory's use of allegorical exegesis, see Abraham J. Malherbe and Everett Ferguson's edition of Gregory of Nyssa's *Life of Moses*, pp. 5-9.) Chrysostom did not use such exegesis. See James W. Cox, "'Eloquent…Mighty in the Scriptures': Biblical Preaching from Chrysostom to Thielicke," *Review and Expositor*, Spring 1975, p. 191. Cox observes, "For Chrysostom the literal meaning of Scripture held sway."

Revelation, all of the New and Old Testaments, in the light of Christ. This has the great benefit of saving us from non-Christological interpretations; in other words, from anti-Christian, including cultic, statements. Moreover, when we see Scripture pointing to Christ and the ultimate fulfillment of his kingdom, we learn something of God's purpose in revelation and history; they head toward meaningful goals.

One more consideration: all parts of Scripture do not strike us as equally meaningful and related to Christ. For example, 2 Chronicles comes across very differently than the Sermon on the Mount. True, 2 Chronicles may in fact come alive at some point down the road, and we had best preach from it when that moment comes, but we can only preach with conviction and authority those texts which come alive in him. In other words, the Grand Source of our inspiration must ignite biblical material before we can expound it.

8. Now come to your conclusions about the meaning of the passage before you.

Ask, What does this passage mean? In the light of your study, record in writing the clear lines of intent.[13]

Next ask specifically, What does this passage have in view for me? What does it mean to my people? What can it mean to my

---

[13]J. J. von Allmen, in his useful paperback, *Preaching and Congregation*, says the first rule for sermon preparation is to identify the main point of the text—the scopus (pp. 53-54). John Henry Newman says, addressing preachers, "Nothing is so fatal to the effect of a sermon as the habit of preaching on three or four subjects at once" (*The Idea of a University*, p. 333). So the interpreter's task is not only to isolate the scopus but to boil it down to a single preachable idea, and to relate all subsidiary meanings to that central meaning.

[14]George A. Turner reminds us that "the expositor's prime task is not only to understand the meaning of the passage but to enter empathetically into the historical situation so completely that he can translate the message of the Scripture from that idiom to one meaningful to his own contemporaries" ("The Interpreter's Task," *Asbury Seminarian*, April 1968, p. 6). A. Purnell Bailey's working principle for preparing sermons and articles is to isolate his own need and to speak and write to that. This, he claims, is a guarantee that he will communicate "on target" (address at the Chaplain's Retreat, Greenham Common, England, November 7, 1978).

congregation? With these questions you begin to make applications and insure the relevance of your interpretation.[14]

At this point in sermon preparation, feel free to test your conclusions against several commentaries. Significant reasons dictate that most of our reading in commentaries should wait until this time; the most important one relates to our conviction that the Holy Spirit and personal experience formulate meanings in examination of the text.[15] To go to commentaries too soon could obstruct the distinctively creative work the Spirit wants to do through us for our people.

You may find yourself under the necessity of doing further study of words, grammatical structures, background, and so on. In any event, arrive now at firm conclusions about the meaning of your chosen Scripture portion, hammering out and perfecting that meaning on paper in concrete terms. Then make it communicable by amplification and illustration in a meaningful sermon manuscript.[16]

Summary

Expositors aim to become contagious about great discoveries. Phillips Brooks writes of the "interpreting power of great enthusiastic men [who] bring out the value of things so that other men can see them."[17] He readily grants that discovery comes hard for

---

[15]Glenn Clark, a professor of creative writing for thirty years, wrote, "I have made a careful and exhaustive study of the sources from whence great writers derive their power. With scarcely a single exception among all the great writers of all time I find that they ascribe their genius to a power outside of themselves." He adds, "Socrates began it when he was announced as 'the wisest of the Greeks because he knew that he knew nothing'" (*Health Through Prayer*, pp. 140-41). Clark goes on to quote George Eliot and Joel Chandler Harris as examples, and shows their dependence on the Higher Power.

[16]John Henry Newman encouraged preachers to write their sermons out in full, not only for the purpose of mastering the material, but also for interpretative reasons: the preacher does not know what he knows, nor does he know his subject, until he actually writes out his material. Newman goes on to say writing keeps the preacher from wandering. See *The Idea of a University*, p. 341.

[17]*The Light of the World and Other Sermons*, p. 327.

some, that appreciation often comes easier. But for preachers this much looms clearly enough: with hard work and goal-oriented concentration, exciting findings emerge. That fact reflects the nature of the human mind and the impact of the Holy Spirit on students of his Word.[18]

---

[18]The literature of preparation, its skills and necessities, is vast. Works like George E. Sweazey's *Preaching the Good News*, David H. C. Read's *Sent from God*, and Warren Wiersbe's *Walking with the Giants* have much to say. William Barclay sums up the urgency of careful preparation in a single question, "Are you studying in such a way that you will make yourself the kind of person for whom life will be a series of open doors?" (*Daily Celebration*, vol. 2, p. 73). Again, see Calvin Miller, *Spirit, Word, and Story: A Philosophy of Marketplace Preaching* (Grand Rapids: Baker, 1996) and *The Empowered Communicator: 7 Keys to Unlocking an Audience* (Nashville: Broadman, 1994).

4

Integration:
Putting It All Together

John Saltmarsh, Vice-Provost of King's College,
Cambridge, in regard to the great fan-vaulted ceiling of
King's College Chapel:
*Sir Christopher Wren used to say that he would undertake
to build just such another—if any man would tell him
where to set the first stone.*

You have done your interpretation homework; your own work, insuring personal integrity. Now you are ready to put the whole sermon together.

Structuring

The preacher, challenged with the task of finding a meaningful arrangement for organizing sermon material, will welcome structural clues.

1. Time may provide a clue to structure.

Imagine yourself working with the two paragraphs of Galatians 4:1-11, and having decided to make the single sentence 4:4 your focal point: "But when the fullness of time had come, God sent his Son, born of a woman, born under the law, in order to redeem those children who were under the law, so that we might receive adoption as children." At once you see Old Testament antecedents implied; also the actual coming of our Lord; finally, significant implications for our lives now. You could then house your material in a construction that communicates (a) the Old Testament prophecy of his coming, (b) his actual coming at a particular point in time, and (c) the present implications of that coming.

Or you may wrestle with the last paragraph of Romans 13:

> [11]Besides this, you know what time it is, how it is now the moment for you to wake from sleep. For salvation is nearer to us now than when we became believers; [12]the night is far gone, the day is near. Let us then lay aside the works of darkness and put on the armor of light; [13]let us live honorably as in the day, not in reveling and drunkenness, not in debauchery and licentiousness, not in quarreling and jealousy. [14]Instead put on the Lord Jesus Christ, and make no provision for the flesh, to gratify its desires.

Your topic might come from verse 11: "Know the Hour," or put in everyday language, "What Time Is It?" Even a quick look at the paragraph shows all three dimensions of time: past, present, and future. But Paul's clear emphasis relates to *now*. What time does the clock say now? It cries: "Wake up!" Why? Because we find ourselves closer to the moment of eternal salvation than when we first believed. He plays on the night and day figure; the night fades quickly, the day will come hurriedly. Paul tells us how to respond in verses 13 and 14, verses which lend themselves to clear application: (a) conduct yourselves becomingly as in the day; (b) put on the Lord Jesus Christ. But Paul does not stop there; he defines becoming conduct and putting on the Lord. So, an outline on the whole paragraph could look like this:

"What Time Is It?"

I. Not night but day.
   A. Day dawns: put on the armor of light.
   B. Night gone: cast off the works of darkness.

II. Day conduct.
   A. Becoming conduct.
      1. Not reveling and drunkenness.
      2 Not debauchery and licentiousness.
      3. Not quarreling and jealousy.
   B. Christ-like conduct.
      1. Put on the Lord Jesus Christ.
      2. Make no provision for the flesh.

That raw, working outline needs refining. One clue to putting it into preachable shape relates to the sequence of commands:

Cast off (v.12).
Put on (v.12).
Put on (v.14).
Make no provision (v.14).

Your broad outline might, then, take this final form:

I. Cast off the works of darkness (Night).
II. Put on the armor of light (Day).
III. Put on the Lord, Jesus Christ (Day).
IV. Make no provision for the flesh (Day and Night contrasted).

Time does indeed sometimes provide a clue to meaningful structuring. You might, at some point, wish to do a series of sermons on God's view of time. Your concordance will help you. And you will make some rich and fruitful discoveries; for example, that the author of Psalm 90 builds the song on the very concept of time.

2. Place may provide the hint to organization.

In Acts 1:8 we have a classic example: Jerusalem (the capital), Judea (the state), Samaria (the adjoining state), and the "ends of the earth" (the world). So here we have an excellent opportunity to preach about the extent of Christian witness: at home, in the surrounding area, further afield, anywhere in the world. Three words could form a working outline out of which your final structure might appear:

Domestic

National

International

The Scriptures make clear the outgoing nature of the gospel. John 7:1 shows Jesus' relationship to both Galilee and Judea; to the former a positive relationship, to the latter a negative. Among other passages which include geographical references, see Deuteronomy 34 which mentions Mount Nebo, Jericho, Dan, Naphtali, Ephraim, Manasseh, Judah, the Western Sea, etc. Psalm 48 refers to "the city of our God," Jerusalem. Endless examples prove the viability of place as a clue to structuring sermons.

3. Persons constitute still another structural indicator.

John 11 affords a good example of this option. Jesus and Lazarus, obviously the key figures, relate meaningfully to Mary, Martha, and the disciples. Note also the new converts, and the unbelieving and opposing Pharisees. Here, by the way, we have an opportunity to work with an entire chapter rather than taking an isolated verse or even a paragraph which could prevent the listener from seeing the picture as a whole. Verse 25, where Jesus says he himself is the resurrection and the life, constitutes the pivot of the chapter. A workable structure could emerge in terms of the simple sequence of the story:

"Jesus the Resurrection"
I. "Lazarus is ill," say Mary and Martha to Jesus (v.3)
II. "Lazarus is dead," says Jesus to his disciples (v.14)
III. "Lazarus, come out!" says Jesus to Lazarus (v.43)
Conclusion: Jesus to Martha: "I am the resurrection and the life" (v. 25).

The marvelous dialogue heard between these three turning points in the narrative gives expression to the changing feelings, attitudes, and perspectives of Mary, Martha, the disciples, and the Jews; finally it shows Jesus' resurrection power which brings life here on earth and in heaven too.

The Acts of the Apostles lends itself to sermons structured around the people in the narrative. Call the people actors; visualize the account as a play. Watch how ideas, housed in the actors, get up and walk and talk and act out meanings. Notice, for example, the chief actors in Acts 9:1-31: Saul ("breathing threats and murder"), the Lord ("Saul, Saul, why do you persecute me?"), Ananias ("Here I am, Lord"), and Barnabas (his name means "Son of encouragement"). Page after page, the twenty-eight chapters of Acts lend themselves to sermons structured around persons, as do vast portions of Holy Writ.

4. Pictures furnish a rich opportunity for making sermon blueprints.

Jesus filled the Sermon on the Mount (Matt. 5-7) with photographs. Christians are salt (5:13) and light (v.14); no one can serve two masters (6:24).

People identify with pictures. When we look at photographs in the family room at home, questions and comments come thick and fast. Pictures stimulate imagination.

Many techniques come to mind for making structural outlines from paintings in Scripture. For example:

a. We can concentrate on individual picture words. Take the paragraph, Luke 6:39-42, where Jesus focuses on the *eye*. In the next paragraph verses 43-45, *heart* becomes significant. In verses 46-49, notice the *ear*: "I will show you what someone is like who comes to me, *hears* my words, and acts on them" (v. 47). Notice that in each case the key word helps us summarize and explain the whole paragraph.

b. Often contrasting picture terms supply hints for sequencing. Thus, in those same three paragraphs, one could work with doublets like this: Luke 6:39-42, *speck* and *log*; 43-45, *figs* and *thorns*; 46-49, *foundations* and *floods*.

c. Sometimes a clear picture can emerge in summarizing sentences. Earlier paragraphs of Luke 6 lend themselves to this kind of structuring. Verses 12-16 could carry the caption, "Jesus prays all night, then chooses his disciples." A heading for verses 20-23 might read, "Luke summarizes the Beatitudes." And the paragraph between, verses 17-19, could, in condensed form, appear like this: "Jesus teaches and heals."

Here, then, we have three techniques for constructing sermons on the basis of pictures presented in Scripture. If you deal with the words *eye*, *heart*, and *foundation* (or *ear*), you might come up with a working outline like this:

   I. The seeing eye.

  II. The pure heart.

 III. The sound foundation.

Or this:

   I. The seeing eye.

  II. The beating heart.

 III. The hearing ear.

Or this:

   I. The perceptive eye.

  II. The productive heart.

 III. The discriminative ear.

Or you might decide to analyze the paragraphs differently, using contrasting terms. "Warnings to Disciples" could serve as the topic, and the structure might appear like this:

 I. Specks and logs.
 II. Thorns or figs.
 III. Foundations and floods.

If you intend to show the relationship of Jesus and his disciples, you might decide to use summarizing sentences:

 I. Jesus prayed, then chose the twelve.
 II. Jesus demonstrated a model ministry for the twelve.
 III. Jesus announced the blessings of discipleship.

Note that in each case pictures become the vehicles of communication. Pictures supply your hearers, conditioned by TV and computer screens, with handles to lay hold of truth.

5. Topical headings may facilitate structuring.

Work once more, by way of example, with the last three paragraphs of Luke 6. A preacher might see verses 39-42 as optical in nature; the next paragraph as horticultural; the final verses, 46-49, as architectural. This kind of structure, a bit more complicated than obvious pictures like eye, heart, and ear, can bring a certain grandeur to the sermon. Adjectival terms may add a grand sound and sophisticated coloration. Assuming both speaker and audience identify with enriched language, the preacher could put into service the following outline, using a title like "The Art of Discipleship":

 I. The optical clue.
 II. The horticultural key.
 III. The architectural design.

Sometimes the sermonizer can couch topical headings in specifically theological terms. Take Psalm 89, for example. Careful study can point to verses 33 and 34 as pivotal to grasping the Psalm.

The steadfast love of God and his faithfulness focus in that great word *covenant*—a strong doctrinal truth. "God Does Keep His Promise" is your theme; you need but two topic heads to support the thesis that God cannot break his word.

  I. God's Never-failing Love.
  II. God's Amazing Faithfulness.

Dress up these words as you will, but that outline could suggest the essence of what you want to say.

Each of the sermon structures we have examined involves a question. Working with time-oriented structuring, the preacher asks, When? Organizing a sermon around place assumes the question, Where? Outlining with reference to persons means asking, Who? Isolating pictures as the basis of arranging material suggests the query, What? So does working with topics, though that type of pattern may also involve questions beginning with Which? and/or How?

Other approaches abound. A cause-and-effect outline, for example, moves logically from one step to another, and implies asking, Why? Still another technique is to spell out a dilemma, then to show its solution. That means asking, How?

A quite different kind of method, outlined in *Principles of Speech Communication*, is Monroe's famous motivational sequence. It follows this pattern: Attention, Need, Satisfaction, Visualization, and Action.[1] Done carefully, this can prove a powerful instrument of persuasion. Capturing attention, showing need, demonstrating fulfillment, pictorializing the thrust of the message, and indicating the lines of action, indicates a technique used in secular as well as sacred speech.

Clearly, creative preachers find many ways to organize a sermon. Often the text lends itself to a particular way, but not necessarily. The speaker's challenge for each sermon is discovering the arrangement best suited for the aim, text, and occasion.

---

[1] See Alan H. Monroe and Douglas Ehringer, *Principles of Speech Communication*, pp. 241-61. Notice especially the diagram on p. 243.

Transitions

Transitions provide a sense of march to the sermon, help to supply the connective tissue which holds the whole address together, and furnish an opportunity to underscore the genuine concerns of your message. How do we go about the task of creating appropriate transitions?

1. Develop a bank of transitional expressions. Examples follow:

First…Second…Third….

First we saw…Next we perceived…Now we notice…

Not only…Not just…But also…

In addition to…Observe that…

Significantly…More importantly…Of most consequence…

Compare this to…Now contrast this to…

The first consideration stimulated this question…

The second factor called to mind this concern…

The third deliberation brings us to a final issue…

Clearly, we must keep the first two items in mind to see the value of the third…

You will notice immediately that transitions can serve not only as bridges but as summaries, thus adding impact to the presentation of the gospel. Interest on a bank account of transitional expressions pays; continuity is the return on your investment.

2. Notice that the shape of the major points assists in transition.

Parallel constructions provide an example. Observe the flow of an outline like this:

 I. Honest business heightens efficiency.
 II. Honest business enhances trust.
 III. Honest business strengthens moral fiber.

You need add only minimal connective tissue to this outline.

Note what happens when you add a contrasting dimension along with connective tissue:

    I. Honest business heightens efficiency; corruption lowers it… and notice too that

    II. Honest business enhances trust; corruption destroys it…now observe that

    III. Honest business strengthens moral fiber; corruption demolishes it.

A cause-and-effect outline can achieve similar transitional goals:

    I. If honesty means business efficiency, and

    II. Honesty gives customers a sense of trust, then

    III. Honesty also strengthens the moral fiber of society.

3. Put in your mental notebook a few things to avoid.

Stay away from vague transitional expressions like:

    Another…
    It could also be that…
    That reminds me of…
    Come to think of it, we should add…

These kinds of signposts, well and good in informal settings, rob sermons of precision, power, and a sense that the minister knows where he or she is going. People listen with purpose when the pulpit speaker communicates the spirit of purpose; transitions show themselves crucial for creating that spirit.

Use these overworked words sparingly:

    Also…
    Then, too…
    Nevertheless…
    By way of contrast…

In other words, master a variety of transitional devices. Variety is the spice of transitional life.

Once more, avoid the nakedness that robs the sermon of that aesthetic dress necessary for providing attractiveness and interest, as it moves from one concern to another. While it is true that one word can serve as a transition—*therefore, moreover, because, however, finally*—usually a little more dress gives the gravity that makes the sermon flow smoothly and helps to maintain interest.

Language

1. Develop your own unique style, the expression of your individuality.[2]

Individuality does not extend to breaking grammatical rules, though some remarkable preachers gave little heed to correctness.[3] For most of us grammar marks the difference between acceptable and unacceptable English, between clearly defined and questionable communication.

Style, relating to pattern of language, involves word selection, phrase construction, sentence arrangement, and all matters of creative, yet appropriate, verbal choice.[4]

Style goes through changes during each preacher's life. It ought to, because the pulpit person constantly changes. He or she learns new vocabulary, discovers fresh ways of putting words and phrases together, and finds better methods of relating one thought to another.

But the evolution builds on a solid stratum of style, the hallmark of the public speaker. That hallmark, fixed in the early years, serves as the language foundation, much as an architect creates his or her

---

[2]George E. Sweazey begins his chapter on style with these straightforward words: "Your style is the way you express yourself, and it is yourself that is being expressed" (*Preaching the Good News*, p. 125). For the wider implications of style, see Mary E. Lyons, "Style" in the *Concise Encyclopedia of Preaching*, pp. 457ff.

[3]Dwight L. Moody, a famous example, pictured on the December 20, 1974 cover of *Christianity Today*, appears in cartoon fashion saying, "If love don't prompt all work, all work is for naught."

[4]In *The Life of John Wesley* (p. 136), John Telford observes, "Wesley's Journals show what a lofty estimate he set on St. John's First Epistle. It was evidently his own model. He expounded it in his Societies; and advised every young preacher to form his style upon it. 'Here,' he says, 'are sublimity and simplicity together, the strongest sense and the plainest language! How could anyone that would "speak as the oracles of God" use harder words than found here?'"

own style built on training in drawing and perspective. What follows will help you construct both the foundation and the developing house.

2. Strive to achieve clarity.

The intentional preacher aims to communicate intended meanings unmistakably. James Black puts it strongly: "Undoubtedly, the first quality we should aim at is clearness."[5] How does the preacher go about achieving communication as clear as fine Swedish crystal?

First, by precision. The preacher-linguist is a technician, a precisionist adept at selecting just the right word.[6] Aim, for example, to put in a single sentence the truth that salvation can change a life. Before you can come up with the clearest possible statement, you may need to play with sentences, working and reworking them, like this:

> *God changes lives.*

That three-word sentence has brevity to commend it, but left alone it comes across vaguely.

> *God changes lives for the better.*

But what does "better" mean?

> *When God changes a life, he does something about sin.*

But what does "something" mean?

> *When God changes a life, he changes it through and through.*

Seasoned Christians, with their conditioned responses, will comprehend the meaning of that sentence, but it still lacks the pre-

---

[5]*The Mystery of Preaching*, p. 103. Louis Cassels, writing to preachers, says, "Whether you are writing or speaking, you cannot make a point unless you are very clear in your own mind what that point is" ("A Consumer of Sermonology Speaks Out," *Christian Herald*, April 1974, p. 27).

[6]Ted Morgan, Frenchman become American, has described his struggle with the English language. What he says about wrestling with our tongue, sweating, straining over it, and "pinning it to the mat," typifies all who work seriously with communication by word. See his "On Becoming American" in *Book Digest*, August 1978, p. 138.

cision required for communication to non-Christians. Experiment. Break down the concept into its component parts:

God

Salvation (change, transformation, healing)

Persons (lives)

Now try your hand at coming up with a sentence that says exactly what you want to communicate:

_____

_____

The second means of achieving clear communication relates to loaded terms. Size up your audience, insofar as possible, in order to avoid emotionally laden terms that raise red flags. While the preacher cannot accommodate his words to each individual in the audience, he or she can define the congregation generally within the lines of theological background, mindset, and culture. But when one works with a vast audience, say over radio or television, or in a church with a healthy cross section of the community, the task becomes more difficult, and the wise preacher selects generalized terms at points where difficulties could arise.

Make a list of troublesome words and acceptable alternatives.[7] Start generally, putting down everything that comes to mind, thus fixing the principle firmly in your thinking.

Girl conveys an image quite different than *chick*.

Gentleman comes across differently than *guy*.

Authority figure makes a different impression than *dictator*.

Now add more refined words to these elementary terms. For example, *young lady* communicates something different than *girl*.

A third way to achieve clarity? Avoid abstract expression. Here the preacher may see the chief problem in achieving clarity. When we use expressions like:

---

[7]See Monroe and Ehringer, *Principles of Speech Communication*, p. 174-76 for a discussion of loaded terms.

> *raising money for a good cause*
> *avoiding evil and choosing good*
> *Puritan work ethic*

people want to know:

> *Specifically, what will the church do with the money?*
> *What evil and good the preacher has in mind?*
> *Who were the Puritans and what is a work ethic?*

When we toss about jargon like:

> *eschatalogical implications*
> *Barth's view of revelation*
> *salvation history*

listeners feel bewildered. Even when we employ more common jargon, like:

> *Paul's doctrine of justification*
> *Wesley's belief in entire sanctification*
> *Our Lord's atonement*

most people still feel at a loss. Interestingly (and sadly), the preacher usually does not know precisely what the expressions mean; jargon easily becomes an escape from defining and crafting.

The good craftsperson reduces abstractions to concrete forms in a conscientious attempt at avoiding ambiguity. Sometimes, we must define terms, though either too frequent or complex definitions succeed in turning down hearing aids all over again. But if, in the interests of careful communication, you must explain a term only vaguely understood, or a word with a double meaning, or a euphemistic expression, then do so briefly. If you preach on salvation, for example, come right out and say it means health, wholeness, healing. Then illustrate its meaning.

3. Use appropriate language.

Language must suit the preacher, the character of the passage expounded, and the church setting.

The preacher is a minister of the gospel. He is a professional and a wordsmith. Dignity of expression precludes the use of slang or adolescent jargon.[8] The minister must use words appropriate to his or her educational level and work.

Not only the preacher, but the passage treated should determine language. If the message signals urgency and intensity, the manner of expression will reflect a high level of seriousness. If, on the other hand, the text aims to comfort, the tenor of the linguistic style will show the supportive presence of God. Clearly, the character and mood of the scriptural unit plays a role in language selection.

Moreover, the church setting itself constitutes a factor in the use of language. The terms used in the church today reflect both traditional and conversational speech. Yes, the move in recent times toward conversational address has entered the house of God. Sloppy speech is never appropriate, nor the opposite extreme, a literary style. How do we characterize *apropos* oral speech? We characterize it by uncomplicated sentence structures, straight-from-the-shoulder approaches, ordinary vocabulary, more monosyllables than polysyllables, humor, and colloquialisms and contractions within reason.[9] The trick, then, lies in marrying language at once possessed of both churchly dignity and winsome appeal.[10]

4. Exercise the stewardship of words.[11]

Oikonomos, the Greek word for "steward," relates to our word *economy*. Our calling requires us to be stewards of language, to use words with judicious care, to pick and choose terms that perform well. That duty compares to the benefits of financial frugality, for carefully honed language communicates with multiplied power

---

[8]Colin Morris, *The Word and the Words*, p. 31, articulates the principle clearly: "The preacher's language ought to reflect the significance of what he is doing, and the dignity of it."

[9]For an interesting discussion supported by experimental research, see Bert E. Bradley, *Fundamentals of Speech Communication: The Credibility of Ideas*, pp. 194-96. Cf. Sweazey, *Preaching the Good News*, pp. 127-28.

[10]Acceptable language for the church is not what some have called "Christianese," a jargon that creates communication problems because it is understood only by insiders.

[11]Note the growing literature on the relations between the Word and words. Three examples: Morris *The Word and the Words*; Sweazey, *Preaching the Good News* (look in the Index under "Words"); Ronald E. Sleeth, "The Recovery of the Word" in "The Crisis in Preaching," *Perkins Journal*, Summer 1977. On the related subject of the philosophy and theories of language see John S. McClure, "Theories of Language" in the *Concise Encyclopedia of Preaching*, pp. 292ff.

even as careful spending allows one to buy high quality products. Economic language comes across as brief, concise, to the point, unencumbered by excess. Neat and clean in address, the speaker prunes away extra words.[12]

Efficiency indicates another component of stewardship. If I use so few words that full meanings do not come through (either cognitively or emotionally) I suffer inefficiency. Thus, on the one hand I dare not get fulsome (that offends), and on the other I must avoid truncated communication. Someone said of John Newton's language that the "fullness and fewness of his words" commended his preaching. A great compliment!

The preacher who strives for economy in language also discovers the difference between boring redundancy on the one hand and creative repetition on the other. "He killed him dead," sounds like a little child—appropriate to the small one, but redundant to an adult. Meaningful repetition, on the other hand, takes a truth and retells it in fresh language and from new perspective. This method, reminiscent of the recurring motif in a Beethoven symphony, appears over and again in new musical forms and thus deepens and enriches meaning. Note, for example, how James S. Stewart does motif preaching (see his book of sermons, *Walking with God*). Themes, though employed many times in Beethoven's and Stewart's works, never come across as boring. The secret? Creative repetition, not mere redundancy.

Exercise stewardship. A genuinely frugal verbal style heightens your powers of communication, and as a fringe benefit teaches your people something about the nature of stewardship in all branches of life.[13]

---

[12]J. J. von Allmen pleads for simplicity in preaching and suggests that its dynamic is love of God's Word and the church (*Preaching and Congregation*, pp. 54-55).

[13]The principle applies to the spiritual life, too. W. Curry Mavis makes precisely this point when he observes that the committed life, in any area, means "selective omissions" (*The Holy Spirit in Christian Life*, p. 1201). Mavis quotes from William

5. Employ pictorial language.

The character, frequency, and aptness of one's figures of speech and illustrations say much about an individual's style. Especially significant for preachers, pictures make the abstract concrete, reveal originality, project emotional substance, and enable the people to comprehend the message.[14]

However, the responsible preacher must face potential problems in pictorial language. For example, over-long illustrations can make time seem to drag. Sometimes the answers to the boredom lie in limiting the number of illustrations, making sure of their freshness,[15] and relating them in economic and exciting language. We must also avoid exaggerated images to make a bigger, better-than-life impression.

The advantages of pictures far outweigh the disadvantages. An illustration has power to bring invigorating perspective; a comparison can throw light on a complex point; a single figure of speech may get right to the heart of a matter, even saving considerable talking time; a story has potential for communicating a truth that would otherwise offend; and a telling image can bring into focus a brand new relationship.

Some preachers use too many illustrations—the so-called "string of pearls" sermonizer does this—but in this telecommunications age, that possibility is fairly remote. The very nature of our language

---

James' *The Varieties of Religious Experience*: "That law which impels the artist to achieve harmony in his composition by simply dropping out whatever jars or suggests a discord, rules also in the spiritual life." Many, including James and Mavis, have referred to the now celebrated quotation from Robert Louis Stevenson: "To omit is the one art in literature. If I knew how to omit, I would ask for no other knowledge."

[14]Dwight L. Moody, taking his cue from the Bible, used many stories, and he told them with strong conviction. See James F. Findlay, Jr., *Dwight L. Moody*, pp. 223ff. James W. Cox, listing Spurgeon's strengths, includes "a wealth of illustrative material" ("'Eloquent…Mighty in the Scriptures': Biblical Preaching from Chrysostom to Thielicke," *Review and Expositor*, Spring 1975, p. 195). See the works of F. Craddock and R. Lewis on the power of picture in the context of narrative or inductive preaching.

[15]Webb B. Garrison, *Taking the Drudgery Out of Sermon Preparation*, pp. 22ff., pleads for freshness and originality, and points out that to use others' stories may not have the same appeal as speaking out of one's own experience.

suggests pictures.[16] The discriminating speaker will use illustrations which vary in type and length.

6. Use active rather than passive language; preach in the present.

Spoken language must communicate an urgent "nowness." When you catch yourself working too much in the past tense, simply change to the present. When you find your subjects acted upon rather than acting, your work needs revising.

How do we achieve present activeness? A rhetorical question may do the trick; it gives the feeling of present involvement to your listeners. Rhetorical questions require no audible answers, but phrased meaningfully get responses from the heart. "Will you now say yes to this challenge?" "Do you see the relevance of Christ to the workplace?" "Have you decided to become a serious disciple of Jesus?"

Another technique: rework sentences. Instead of saying, "Lazarus was sick and died, and Jesus raised him from the dead," say, "Sick, yes; dead, yes; but Jesus, alive to Lazarus's need, comes to Lazarus's rescue." The sense of immediacy in the reworked sentence supplies life and breath to the old, old story.

Make sentences active, fresh, vigorous. You may wish to study models of preachers who have learned the art. When you do, note how their style possesses a sense of drama which makes gospel truth come alive.[17]

Summary

Style, a many-splendored thing, defies complete definition. Far more goes into it than meets the eye of the casual observer; it reflects

---

[16]The poets of all ages worked intimately with images. Observe what awakened Dylan Thomas to the glorious possibilities of the English language: nursery rhymes, folk tales, Scottish ballads, lines from hymns, Bible stories, the rhythm of the Bible, Blake's *Songs of Innocence* (see *Poet in the Making: The Notebooks of Dylan Thomas*, p. 12).

[17]Listen to Chuck Swindoll. Read James S. Stewart, *The Wind of the Spirit*, and his other books of sermons. See also *Great Preaching: Evangelical Messages by Contemporary Christians*, eds. Sherwood Eliot Wirt and Viola Blake.

your personality. But you cannot go wrong by working diligently toward achieving language that is clear, appropriate, economical (reflecting the responsible stewardship of words), pictorial, and energetic.

5

Authority:
Three Crucial Components

"One thing and one thing only sets the preacher
apart from the rest of men: he is assumed to
speak with authority on matters of the spirit."
—Webb B. Garrison, *Taking the Drudgery*
out of Sermon Preparation, p. 25

We come now to an altogether significant issue—significant for communication and, more particularly, for gospel communication. Pulpit success pivots on authority. How does personal, spiritual authority become reality?

The Authority of the Preacher

Of special significance to the congregation is their minister.[1] He or she stands as God's representative. Yes, the people want to hear from great authorities,[2] but even renowned men and women will take on significance only in proportion to the confidence the hearers have in their own minister. What ingredients, then, make the minister truly authoritative?

---

[1]Paul Scherer, in Chapter 2, "Like a Man of God," of his Yale Lectures, says, "…from the manner of man he [the preacher] shall ever be drawn the true quality and reach of his power" (*For We Have This Treasure,* p. 32). See also David L. Bartlett, "Authority" in the *Concise Encyclopedia of Preaching,* p. 22-3.

[2]Alan H. Monroe and Douglas Ehringer (*Principles of Speech Communication,* p. 120) list the tests of authority as two: pertinence and audience acceptability. They go on

1. Good character marks the authoritative preacher.[3]

A bishop's unsportsmanlike behavior after losing at tennis once disillusioned one of God's "little ones."[4] For the "little one," the bishop had momentarily lost his authority as a gospel communicator. W. Curry Mavis puts the truth at hand positively and succinctly: "Good character prepares the way for effective communication."[5] True, none of us behaves consistently all the time, but our people will sense the thrust and motivation of our lives. What people discern determines, in a real sense, the measure of our authority.

Do I come across as a biblical person?[6] The minister who courageously comes to terms with this question grows in authoritative communication.

2. The authoritative minister shows dedication.

Singularity of purpose characterizes the preacher faithful to his or her calling. To play at ministry—such a sin!—robs one of authority. Can you even conceive of a Rubens, a da Vinci, or a Raphael doing a kind of child's painting and presenting it to the public as a serious work? Can you think of Rodin, Moore, or Michelangelo producing a

---

to indicate four other specific criteria with references to authorities quoted: (1) "The person quoted should be qualified by training and experience, as an authority." (2) When possible, "the statement of the authority should be based on firsthand knowledge." (3) In the interests of avoiding prejudice, "the judgment expressed should not be unduly influenced by personal interest." (4) "The hearers should realize that the person quoted actually is an authority."

[3]Cf. relevant materials in Chapter 1.

[4]The "little one" was Dick Sheppard who eventually became the pastor of St. Martin-in-the-Fields, London. Sheppard remarked, "As an undergraduate I lost for a time what little faith I had because I saw a bishop unable to take a beating at tennis like a gentleman." Sheppard went on to admit his "poor faith," but insisted that if a leader behaves "like a cad when he loses a game, it is a bad outlook for the rest of us" (John W. Doberstein, ed., *Minister's Prayer Book*, p. 275).

[5]*The Holy Spirit in the Christian Life*, p. 130.

[6]Elton Trueblood has a forthright word on this point, a word that applies to preachers as well as laypersons: "The Bible can be of real aid only if the reader has within himself the experiences to which the Biblical writers point" (*The Meditations of Elton Trueblood*, eds. Stephen Sebert and Gordon Ross, p. 52).

sloppy sculpture? The majestic care which characterizes their work marks their unalloyed devotion to their art.

The minister of God who does homework with that kind of consecration will inevitably command the respect of his or her people. That preacher's name may never travel much beyond local circles (though very often people out and about hear well enough), but fame can carry precious little weight with individual congregants. The passion of the dedicated pastor's heart relates only to establishing authority that will open the ears of the people, and thus bring them the help they need.

Human beings respect hard-working dedication. Not artificially labored ("I am trying like mad"), but the devotion that confidently produces a sure word from the Lord Sunday by Sunday.[7] That kind of serious intention captures respect and therefore authority.

3. The authoritative preacher empathizes with the congregation.

On any given Sunday morning a good percentage of our people face difficult challenges. They fight for grace to live with impossible people, illnesses, and unhappy financial pictures. They wrestle to find sufficient energy and creativity to get their work done and done with satisfaction. They want to find answers and meaning in the humdrum of life.

The easygoing manner of some people—the lightheartedness of youth; preoccupation with the new car, the new baby, or the new boat—makes it appear that God's in his heaven and all's right with the world. The facts tell us something different: most people fight battles they seldom, sometimes never, discuss. The minister who, by manner, says, "I care. I'm available if you need me," has hit a home run with hurting people. Of course they will listen to that preacher!

---

[7] In 2 Timothy 2:15 ("Do your best to present yourself to God as one approved by him, a worker who has no need to be ashamed, rightly explaining the word of truth") Paul admonishes Timothy to develop a spirit of unmistakable intentionality.

Empathy does not come easily for the preacher. It did not for Moses. When his people complained, he pleaded, dealt, and wept with them. He found the business of understanding what festered underneath their surface rebellion difficult. Beneath their disobedience lay hurting hearts.

So it is in our work today. A church officer feels slighted because, at the dedication of the new church building, he did not find himself included amongst the dignitaries in public view; his picture did not appear in the local press with his colleagues. He deserved recognition! After all, hadn't he helped on the project from the first? Hadn't he invested long hours? Hadn't he solved the problems that seemed for all the world insoluble? Now slighted, he resigns his church post, wounded and inconsolable. The wise pastor aches with him. Together they wrestle and pray and hope. Finally, resolution comes, but not without the pain of pastoral involvement. And that very pain puts a new content into the pastor's preaching. Not that he so much as hints at the wounded feelings behind the scenes, and certainly not that he ever "preaches at" the wounded officer. But that the pathos in the preaching, both in context and style, reflects new insight into the difficulties of human existence. The congregation detects the sensitivity of the preacher almost immediately.

St. Paul speaks very personally to the Galatians, clearly empathizing with them: "My little children, for whom I am again in the pain of childbirth until Christ is formed in you, I wish I were present with you now..." (Gal. 4:19-20a).

4. The authoritative minister emphasizes the positive.

Herbert H. Clark, Johns Hopkins psychologist, discovered that people take 48 percent longer to comprehend negative sentences than positive ones.[8] The affirming preacher gets through; the habitually negative pulpiteer turns down hearing aids.

---

[8]See Michael Korda, *Success!* as condensed in *Book Digest*, August 1978. pp. 171-72. See also Gary Dorsey's break-through findings in "Latest Therapy: Accenting the Positive," *Lexington Herald-Leader*, 23 June 2000, A9.

Concentrating on what the gospel does, instead of on what people shouldn't do, is the secret. To emphasize the law overmuch is negative preaching (that sometimes must be done, but it takes extra effort); the New Testament proclamation emphasizes grace.[9]

Relating how Franklin Roosevelt overcame polio or Moses succeeded against impossible odds commands a hearty response. To say, "When we do…," rather than "If we can't…," helps people rise to the challenge. Human nature responds to *can*, *do*, and *will*, but recoils from *not sure*, *probably can't*, and *rather doubtful*.

The minister who wishes to move amongst his people with authority, will assume a positive rather than a negative posture in speech, yet not recoil from prophetic utterance when called by God and his Word to do so.

5. The authoritative preacher delivers sermons with confidence.

William Shakespeare has a downright funny passage in Hamlet, humorous because the playwright exposes the inept speaker: "Speak the speech I pray you, as I pronounced it to you, trippingly on the tongue; but if you mouth it as many of your players do, I had as lief the towncrier spoke my lines. Nor do not saw the air too much with your hand, thus: but use all gently" (*Hamlet*, III, ii, 1).

The bard says it all: master flow, exercise economy, articulate, don't yell, use body language appropriately. Modern research tells us that a direct correlation exists between public speaking and leadership. Clearly, good public speaking and authority go together. Preparation, voice and diction, personal appearance, kinesics, adaptation to the audience, eye contact and freedom from notes— all of these and more factor into communicable pulpit address.[10]

---

[9]John Wesley taught that we must preach law before grace. But let us not forget that even in communicating law we must come sooner or later to its great benefits; and once that gets through, let us not dwell on it unnecessarily, but move on to grace.

[10]Classical rhetoric followed a five step procedure, delivery appearing last: (1) Invention—finding what to say; (2) Disposition—arranging; (3) Style—suitable language; (4) Memory—mastering material; (5) Delivery—putting it across.

The Authority of the Spirit

Undeniably, authority in preaching comes from the present and active Spirit of God, in the preaching itself and in the hearing of the Word.[11] Every authentic preacher knows the reality of the Spirit's presence in preaching.[12] Sometimes the preacher stands in the pulpit unaware of the Spirit's activity; sometimes he or she misreads the Spirit; never does the proclaimer come close to full awareness of the Spirit of God's communicating strength. Yet the spiritually alert preacher has some sense of the living Lord in the spoken word.

What lets the Spirit loose in our preaching?

1. Prayer plays a vital role.

The Spirit draws us to our knees first and foremost by our humanity. Our definite need tells us we have no choice but to come to him. He is the true source of strength, comfort, and help.[13] He alone knows what he wants to say through his servant.

When we get quiet enough to hear his voice, he speaks. He may tell us something specific to preach next Sunday or a month from

---

[11]Peter Torry observes that "when a pastor believes God is speaking as he preaches, confidence returns to the pulpit, and life flows from God. God is heard. He is present. The apathy of the people is dealt with when God speaks" ("The Mystery and Power of Preaching," *Christianity Today*, 22 September 1978, pp. 30-31).

[12]J. J. von Allmen believes the Holy Spirit accompanies true preaching (*Preaching and Congregation*, p.31). Moreover, "God is not so much the object as the true source of Christian preaching. Preaching is thus speech by God rather than speech about God." Thus, "our role is not that of the impresario presenting a star to the crowd" (p. 7). Stanley N. Gundry, in "Grand Themes of D. L. Moody," reminds us of Moody's 1871 crisis which unleashed the Spirit in his preaching and caused him to say such things as, "It is not our work to make them believe. That is the work of the Spirit. Our work is to give them the Word of God" (*Christianity Today*, 20 December 1974, p. 5).

[13]Note what Robert J. White, the brain surgeon, says about prayer as a resource. Writing in *Reader's Digest* for September 1978, he says (p. 100), "I pray a great deal, especially before and after surgery." He finds prayer "satisfying" and believes "immense resources" support him. Cf. A. T. Robertson's statement, "The secret of success in the ministry is very simple. It is real connection with God, vital union with Christ" (quoted by Warren Wiersbe, *Walking with the Giants*, p. 258). Again, hear Harold Lindsell: "The very best preparation for preaching is prayer" (*When You Pray*, p.19). On the same page, Lindsell says, "The finest homiletical production is powerless without prayer."

now, what illustration to call into service, what line of thought to follow under a heading. Other times he has no specific message at all; he simply wants us to get saturated with him, for the Spirit in the preacher does the business of gospel communication.[14]

James S. Stewart summed up the urgency of prayer, in a single sentence, with reference to an historic Scottish preacher: "Chalmers was indeed going to the root of the matter when he declared that most failures in the ministry were due, not to lack of visiting or of study or of organizational activity, but to lack of prayer."[15]

2. Acknowledge the Spirit of God as sovereign in the communication of his Word (1 Cor. 2:12-13; 1 Thess. 2:13).

The preacher can save no one; only God saves. This acknowledgment results in great relief for the preacher, for so long as he carries the burden of saving the lost and nurturing the saved, he lifts a weight too heavy for himself. Indeed, God never made us to shoulder such a load.

To hoist that burden inevitably ends in tragedy. Thus, the evangelist who has learned to manipulate human emotions ends up with stillbirths instead of new births. The pastor counseling smugly from the pulpit sooner or later finds his advice turning to vice. The preacher who treats spiritual matters with slick urbanity gets lavish compliments at the door and perhaps little else.

Pride says, "I can do the job myself." The man of God knows very well he can do nothing of the sort. The humble preacher acknowledges deep inside him or herself that gospel communication is the special province of God. To know and believe that sincerely means cooperating with God who lets loose his Spirit upon the people; the Authority himself stands free to do his grand work.

---

[14]Karl Barth held that "because...preaching is, by definition, concerned solely with God, it is not possible to preach without praying that the words spoken may become the call of God to men; and, moreover, the whole congregation should join in this prayer" (*Prayer and Preaching*, p. 98).

[15]*Heralds of God*, p. 202.

3. The church also serves to loose the Spirit in preaching.

The church at worship prays to the Lord and acknowledges the sovereignty of the Spirit, and thus allows him to open doors to receiving messages on the part of his people. God enters humble hearts; truly to pray, truly to acknowledge God, invites the grace of humility.

Preaching and listening in the context of worship constitute the bases of fellowship. God speaks in the fellowship. In church we often hear things we cannot seem to hear any other time. He comes specially to the fellowship, ready to unplug ears to hear him announce a supreme Word tailored to individual and kingdom ends.

The church, by the power of the Spirit, gives authority to the preacher for gospel declaration. Ordination, pastoral appointment, the very presence of worshipers in a service all say, "The church authorizes the preacher to speak for God." Thus, the pulpit has potential for the proclamation of truth with power. Moreover, the preacher does not stand alone as he speaks; the great body of believers, past, present, and future, join him or her. The preacher, in fact, represents the church universal and eternal; thus, his or her faithfulness to the Word recorded in the Bible, living in the risen Christ, spoken in gospel proclamation.

The Authority of the Bible

Confined to the speaker, authority would lack the strength of God's Spirit. To objectify truth, God provides his Word. Thus with the speaker's authority and the authority of the Holy Spirit, God supplies a third component, the written record of his revelation.

The Bible provides ultimate truth. Indeed, the Scriptures[16] constitute the great repository of unyielding, divine truth, and as such constitute the authority against which we test our ideas.[17]

---

[16]Swiss reformer Zwingli not only encouraged his hearers to follow Christ's command to search the Scriptures, but felt so strongly that he preached with the intent "that the Scriptures might be forcibly brought to the notice of those ignorant of the same" ("Choice and Free Use of Foods" in *Twenty Centuries of Great Preaching*, eds. William M. Pinson, Jr., and Clyde E. Fant, Jr., vol. 2, p. 122).

[17]D. Martyn Lloyd-Jones speaks of the results of making oneself an authority in place of the Bible: "Man put himself in the position of authority and turned down the

How, then, does God make the Scriptures authoritative?

1. The Bible works.

Listen to Smiley Blanton's answer to the question, "Do you, a psychiatrist, read the Bible?" The question was asked by a new patient who saw a Bible on Dr. Blanton's desk. He listened intently, no doubt, to the famous practitioner's answer: "I not only read it, I study it. It's the greatest textbook on human behavior ever put together. If people would absorb its message, a lot of us psychiatrists could close our offices and go fishing."[18]

The great evangelists like Dwight L. Moody, Billy Sunday,[19] and Billy Graham preach with the assumption the Bible works. "The Bible says," no mere formula with Graham, acts as the considered preface to a firm and fixed statement of truth, a statement that reverberates with life.[20]

Graham did not come to his position easily. In a significant article, "Biblical Authority in Evangelism," he confesses the struggles

authority of God; and we today are reaping the consequences of that. God, as it were, turns to mankind and says: Very well, I will just allow you to see what your philosophies lead to" ("Beginning to Understand" in *Twenty Centuries of Great Preaching*, vol. 11, p. 304).

John Wesley declared, "The Scriptures are the touchstone whereby Christians examine all, real and supposed, revelations. In all cases, they appeal 'to the law and to the testimony,' and try every spirit thereby" (*The Letters of the Rev. John Wesley*, ed. John Telford, vol. 2, p. 117). Cf. Billy Graham: "I use the phrase, 'The Bible says,' because the Word of God is the authoritative basis of our faith" ("Biblical Authority in Evangelism," *Christianity Today*, 15 October 1956, p. 7).

[18]Quoted by Frank Bateman Stanger, "The Healing Power of Love: What Better Medicine Is There?" *The Herald*, July/August 1978, p. 13.

[19]Says Billy Sunday in his sermon on the "Second Coming of Christ," "Instead of going to the Bible to find out what God says, the preacher is too apt to go to his books, to see what the great men of his church have to say about it, and all their preaching and teaching takes its color from the glasses the rabbis wear, just as was the case in the time of Jesus" (*Twenty Centuries of Great Preaching*,. vol. 7, p. 266). Henry Ward Beecher, a quite different kind of preacher, said regarding the authority of the Bible, "The Scripture itself insists upon the validity on account of its moral power." Again, "the authority of truth is that it is true" (*Ibid.*, vol. 9, pp. 343–44).

[20]Ralph L. Lewis compared Graham and the prophet Amos: Amos "recites the refrain 54 times, 'thus saith the Lord,' or 'the Lord said' (as Billy Graham does in our day)" ("Four Preaching Aims of Amos," *Asbury Seminarian*, April 1967, p. 16).

he had in 1949, and reveals how he won a crucial battle over doubt. In the same article, Graham relates the exciting emergence of authority in his preaching. Within six weeks of his acceptance of the total reliability of the Bible, he began the now historic Los Angeles campaign where "I discovered the secret that changed my ministry. I stopped trying to prove that the Bible was true. I had settled in my own mind that it was, and this faith was conveyed to the audience. Over and over again I found myself saying 'The Bible says.' I felt as though I were merely a voice through which the Holy Spirit was speaking." Now listen: "Authority created faith. Faith generated response, and hundreds of people were impelled to come to Christ."[21]

The pragmatism of Scripture goes beyond the visible response in an evangelistic setting. *Decision*, Graham's official mass circulation publication, ran a long series of articles entitled, "Where Are They Now?" Each piece tells the story of someone saved in a Graham campaign years before, who currently serves Christ and his church.[22] The Spirit and the Word do indeed possess power to save and sustain.

What more could we say about the pragmatism of the Bible? The Ten Commandments work. So does 1 Corinthians 13. The Sermon on the Mount functions with astonishing effectiveness when put into operation by the power of God's Spirit. The workability of

---

[21]Graham, "Biblical Authority in Evangelism," *Christianity Today* (15 Oct. 1956, pp. 5-6). The authority of Christ, in both preaching and Scripture, preachers often discuss. G. Campbell Morgan, in his book, *Preaching*, declares "a sermon should be characterized also by authority" (p. 40). Quoting Matthew 7:28–29, he works with the expression, "[Jesus taught] as one having authority, not as their scribes." Morgan shows the difference between the two authorities. The nature of the scribes' authority lies in "their recognized position" (p. 43); they had been as interpreters of Moses' law. Morgan sees Christ's authority not primarily in His demeanor, attitude, or look. "His authority was rather the authority of the thing He said" (p. 44). Note, for example, the Sermon on the Mount: "Human consciousness never quarrels with it" (p. 44). R. W. Dale speaks in terms different but complementary to Morgan: "Men are subjects of Christ by the Divine will, though it lies with their own will to determine whether they will be obedient to His laws and loyal to His throne" (*Twenty Centuries of Great Preaching*, vol. 5, p. 169).

[22]E.g., "The Story of M. S. Scott," *Decision*, August 1978, p. 11.

biblical truth in all its expressions finds documentation a thousand times and in as many ways. The statement, "Thy Word is truth," has the solid backing of experiential religion.

2. The Scriptures communicate God himself.

The power behind the pragmatic effectiveness of the Word is God himself. In the Bible God talks.[23]

True expository preaching means speaking for God, not ourselves.[24] That explains why we need not pepper our utterances with "I think," "perhaps," and "maybe." We do indeed employ conditional language when we speak on our own (as St. Paul did on occasion), or when we feel unsure of an interpretation—the exception for men and women convinced of the truth of God's Word.

Almighty God himself is in his Word, the most fundamental truth any preacher can lay hold of. God uses preachers who see the Bible as his Word. God uses them so men and women, boys and girls, can come alive and know wholeness. In a word, the Almighty honors his message faithfully articulated through his servants.

But we must go deeper. The power of the Bible reveals God not only in what he does, but in how he gives himself in his Word. If one wishes to catch the spirit of a great painter, he had best study the drawings, sketches, and paintings themselves.[25] If a minister wishes to imbibe the Spirit of God, what better way than study of the primary Source?[26] Advancing knowledge of God, the necessary

---

[23]The Reformers held that all authority rests in God: Luther, for example, in his sermon, "The Third Sunday After Trinity"; John Knox also in "The Source and Bounds of Kingly Power" (*Twenty Centuries of Great Preaching,* vol. 2, pp. 37 and 211).

[24]William B. Coker, in a fiery and moving editorial, "Prophetic Succession," says of the prophet-preacher, "To speak for God becomes the ambition of his life; all else is secondary. To speak for God is his assignment; any other appointment is subordinate.... He speaks not for himself; not in his name nor in the name of any other, man or institution; he speaks for God" (*Asbury Seminarian*, January 1970, p. 4).

[25]One can, in fact, do this. E.g., the British Museum, London makes available to researchers actual drawings of Michelangelo, Gainsborough, Reynolds, *et al.*

[26]Peter Rhea Jones says, "When the preaching minister is captivated by the original meaning of a Scripture passage he may very well proclaim with authority" ("Biblical Hermeneutics," *Review and Expositor*, Spring 1975, p. 144). Jones advises students of exegesis to try to put the intention of scriptural texts into a single sentence.

precursor of all spiritual growth, brings increased authority and heightened pulpit power.

Summary

Sources of the preacher's authority include the speaker, the Holy Spirit, and the Bible. As for the speaker, good character, dedication, empathy, positive emphasis, and good delivery all come in for consideration. Consistent biblical behavior is basic to good character;[27] singularity of purpose the key to dedication; capacity to identify with others beneath surface levels the secret of telling empathy; positive announcement, as against negative pronouncement, the guide to proper emphasis, even heightened delivery skills.

Gospel communication is a special province of the Holy Spirit. He wants to work in the contexts of prayer, acknowledgment of his sovereignty, and the church. Our humanity dictates the necessity of prayer, openness to the inner voice and to God himself. To recognize God's Spirit as sovereign releases one from unbearable concern for success, and contributes to unleashing the Spirit's power. The church, a unique forum for the Spirit's messages, provides fellowship which opens the door to conversation with God, others, and oneself. Moreover, the church, vested with power to give authority to God's ordained gospel transmitters, acts as heaven's vehicle for communication.

The Bible provides authority to and through God's preachers in the context of genuine faith. With the authority of God's Word the preacher speaks a confident, and therefore belief-building word; that word bears fruit in transformed lives. Moreover, God communicates himself in the exposition of his Word, and therein lies the grand goal of preaching.

---

[27]Money, sex, and power, the three classic stumbling blocks, come in for their share of treatment in the literature. E.g., Richard Foster's well known work, originally titled *Money, Sex and Power*, carries the sub-title *The Challenge of the Disciplined Life* (Harper, 1985). See also the *Christianity Today* issue on money (June 12, 2000).

APPENDIX

100 Books for the Preacher's Library
With Alternative Suggestions

I. Bibles:

1. *Reflecting God Study Bible* (NIV). Grand Rapids: Zondervan, 2000. From the Wesleyan theological perspective.

The Holman Study Bible (Revised Standard Version). Philadelphia: A.J. Holman Company, 1962.

The Holman Thin Reference Bible NRSV (1990).

NRSV *Harper Study Bible* (1991)

The Message: The New Testament in Contemporary English, tr. by Eugene H. Peterson. Colorado Springs, CO: Navpress, 1993. (See also Peterson's *Message* for Psalms and Proverbs. Currently, he works on completing the O.T.)

2. *The Eight Translation New Testament*: KJV, Living, Phillips, RSV, TEV, NIV, JB, NEB. Wheaton: Tyndale, 1974.

The Precise Parallel New Testament: Greek, KJV, Rheims, Amplified, NIV, NRSV, NAB, NASB. John R. Kohlenberger III, General Editor. New York: Oxford, 1995.

The Comparative Study Bible: NIV, NAS, AB, KSV, 1984.

3. *The RSV Interlinear Greek-English New Testament* by Alfred Marshall. Grand Rapids: Zondervan, 1970 edition with a foreword by J.B. Phillips.

The Septuagint with Apocrypha: Greek and English. Hendrickson, 1998, (7th printing).

4. *The Hebrew-English Old Testament.* London: Samuel Bagster and Sons, Ltd., 1971.

5. *The Greek New Testament* edited by Kurt Aland, Matthew Black, Carlo M. Martini, Bruce M. Metzger, and Allen Wikgran in cooperation with the Institute for New Testament Textual Research. Third edition corrected 1983 published in London by the United Bible Societies.

II. Concordances:

6. *Nelson's Complete Concordance of the Revised Standard Version* (1957). New York: Thomas Nelson and Sons, and compiled under the supervision of John W. Ellison.

John R. Kohlenberger III, *The NRSV Concordance Unabridged.* Zondervan, 1991. Includes Apocrypha and Deutero-Canonical books.

Richard E. Whitaker and John R. Kohlenberger III, *The Analytical Concordance to the New Revised Standard Version of the New Testament.* Grand Rapids: Wm. B. Eerdmans Publishing Company, 2000.

See also Clinton Morrison, *An Analytical Concordance to the RSV of the NT.* Philadelphia: Westminster, 1979.

If you prefer the NIV, use Edward W. Goodrick and John R. Kohlenberger III, *The NIV Complete Concordance.* Grand Rapids: Zondervan, 1981.

You should make yourself aware of *The Complete Concordance to the Bible: New King James Version.* Nashville: Thomas Nelson Publishers, 1983.

Also David Robinson and L. Jane Rowley, *Concordance to the Good News Bible.* Nashville: Thomas Nelson, 1983.

For KJV: *Young's Analytical Concordance* (Eerdmans, 1970); *Strong's Exhaustive Concordance* (Abingdon, 1986).

7. A topical concordance such as *Holman's* (Nashville), which includes subjects, themes and doctrines all indexed.

R.D. Hitchcock, *Baker's Topical Bible* (1975).

Also C.R. Joy, Jr., *Harper's Topical Concordance* (1962).

A. Colin Day, *Roget's Thesaurus of the Bible*. San Francisco: Harper Collins, 1992.

Nelson's Concordance of Bible Phrases. Nashville: Thomas Nelson, 1992.

8. *Subject Guide to Bible Stories*. New York: Greenwood Publishing Corporation, 1969. Done by George Frederick Garland. Includes both a subject and persons guide.

III. Lexicons:

9. Walter Bauer, *et al*, *A Greek-English Lexicon of the New Testament and Other Early Christian Literature*. Chicago: University of Chicago Press, 2nd and augmented edition, 1979.

Note the convenient Alexander Souter, *Pocket Lexicon to the Greek New Testament*. New York: Oxford University Press, 1916.

10. William Gesenius, tr. by Edward Robinson and edited by Francis Brown, S.R. Driver, and Charles A. Briggs, *A Hebrew and English Lexicon of the Old Testament*. New York: Oxford University Press, corrected edition, 1953.

Or B. Davidson, *The Analytical Hebrew and Chaldee Lexicon*. Grand Rapids: Zondervan, first printing, 1970.

IV. Gospel Harmonies:

11. Kurt Aland, ed., *Synopsis of the Four Gospels*. London: United Bible Societies, 3rd edition, 1979. Includes Greek and English, and puts the Gospel accounts side by side.

Huck-Lietzman, *Gospel Parallels: A Synopsis of the First Three Gospels* edited by Burton H. Throckmorton, Jr. and published by Thomas Nelson of Nashville, 4th edition, 1979.

Also, Thomas & Gundry, *Harmony of the Gospels-NIV*. Harper, 1988.

Or, O. Daniel, *A Harmony of the Four Gospels*. Baker, 1986.

V. Word Books

Including Theological Dictionaries, etc.

12. Geoffrey W. Bromiley, editor, *Theological Dictionary of the New Testament*, originally edited by Gerhard Kittel and Gerhard Friedrich translated by Geoffrey W. Bromiley: Abridged in One Volume. Grand Rapids: Eerdmans, 1985. This revised and abridged edition of the multi-volume Kittel is a money, time, and space saver for the preacher.

13. Alan Richardson, *A Theological Word Book of the Bible*. London: SCM, 1950 (now available in paperback).

14. William Barclay, *New Testament Words* (brings together *A New Testament Wordbook* and *More New Testament Words*, Philadelphia: Westminster, 1976 reprint.

15. Richard S. Taylor, ed., *Beacon Dictionary of Theology*. Kansas City: Beacon Hill Press, 1983.
See too, Gordon S. Wakefield, ed., *The Westminster Dictionary of Christian Spirituality*. Philadelphia, 1983.

16-18. Colin Brown, ed., *The New International Dictionary of New Testament Theology*. Grand Rapids: Zondervan, 1976-79. Scripture Index vol. by David Townsley and Russell Bjork. (1985).
See also Robin Keeley, Organizing Editor, *Eerdmans' Handbook to Christian Belief*, 1982.

19. Walter A. Elwell, ed., *Evangelical Dictionary of Biblical Theology*. Grand Rapids: Baker, 1996.
See also Sinclair B. Ferguson and David F. Wright, eds., and J.I. Packer, consulting ed., *New Dictionary of Theology*. Downers Grove, IL: IVF, 1988.
See too, Daniel G. Reid, Coordinating Ed., *Dictionary of Christianity in America*. Downers Grove, IL: IVF, 1990.

VI. Bible Dictionaries and Encyclopedias:

20. J. D. Douglas, Ed., *The New Bible Dictionary*. Wheaton: Tyndale, 1982 (revised).

Eerdmans' Bible Dictionary. Grand Rapids: Eerdmans, 1987.

Lawrence O. Richards, ed., *The Revell Bible Dictionary.* Grand Rapids: Revell, 1992.

D.N. Freedman, ed., *The Anchor Bible Dictionary.* N.Y.: Doubleday: 1992, 6 vols.

Derek Williams, ed., *New Concise Bible Dictionary.* Downers Grove: InterVarsity Press, 1989.

Bromiley, G.W., ed., *International Standard Bible Encyclopedia.* 4 vols. Grand Rapids: Eerdmans, 1979-88.

21-25. Merrill C. Tenney, ed., *The Zondervan Pictorial Encyclopedia of the Bible.* 5 vols. Grand Rapids: Zondervan, 1976.

See also the one-volume *Eerdmans' Concise Bible Encyclopedia,* 1980.

Gleason Archer, ed., *Encyclopedia of Bible Difficulties.* Grand Rapids: Zondervan, 1982. Contains three indices: persons, subjects, references.

Larry Richards, *Bible Difficulties Solved.* Grand Rapids: Revell, 1993.

J. I. Packer, *et. al., Nelson's Illustrated Encyclopedia of Bible Facts.* Nashville: Nelson, 1995.

26. T. A. Bryant, in association with others, *Today's Dictionary of the Bible.* Minneapolis: Bethany, 1982.

Note: A number of Bible dictionaries have come off the press in recent years. Examples:

P. J. Achtemeier, ed., *Harper's Bible Dictionary.* 1985.

Lawrence O. Richards, *Expository Dictionary of Bible Words.* Grand Rapids: Zondervan, 1985.

Lawrence O. Richards, *Dictionary of Basic Bible Truths.* Grand Rapids: Zondervan, 1987.

Unger's Concise Bible Dictionary with Complete Pronounciation Guide to Bible Names. Grand Rapids: Baker, 1987.

The Revell Bible Dictionary. Grand Rapids: Revell, 1990.

Derek Williams, *New Concise Bible Dictionary.* Wheaton: Tyndale, 1989.

J.D. Douglas and Merrill C. Tenney, *The New International Dictionary of the Bible*. Grand Rapids: Zondervan, 1987.

Nelson's Illustrated Bible Dictionary. Nashville: Nelson, 1986.

Exegetical Dictionary of the NT, Vol. 1, ed. by H. Batz and Gerhard Schneider. Grand Rapids: Eerdmans, 1990.

Trent C. Butler, Ed., *Holman Bible Dictionary*. Nashville: Broadman and Holman: 1991.

Joel B. Green and Scot McKnight, eds., *Dictionary of Jesus and the Gospels*. Downers Grove: IVF, 1992.

Ronald F. Youngblood, Gen. Ed., *Nelson's New Illustrated Bible Dictionary*. Nashville: Nelson, 1995.

VII. Bible Atlases, Geographies, Handbooks:

27. Y. Aharoni, *The Land of the Bible: A Historical Geography*. Philadelphia: Westminster, 1967.

George A. Turner, *Historical Geography of the Holy Land*. Grand Rapids: Baker, 1973.

Student Manual: Historical Geography of the Bible Lands. Grand Rapids: Zondervan, 1979.

Denis Baly, *Basic Biblical Geography*. Philadelphia: Fortress, 1987.

28. *Eerdmans' Atlas of the Bible: With A-Z Guide to Place*. Grand Rapids: Eerdmans, 1983.

Barry J. Beitzel, *The Moody Atlas of Bible Lands*. Chicago: Moody Press, 1985.

The New Bible Atlas. Downers Grove: IVF, 1985.

The Holman Bible Atlas. Nashville: Holman, 1978.

Harper's Atlas of the Bible. New York: Harper and Brothers, 1987.

The Macmillan Bible Atlas. New York: Macmillan,1993.

New Bible Atlas. Downers Grove: IVF, 1985.

Rand McNally Bible Atlas . New York: Rand McNally, n.d.

The Zondervan NIV Atlas of the Bible: Grand Rapids: Zondervan, 1989.

John Rogerson, *Atlas of the Bible*. New York: Facts on File, 1991.

29. Lawrence O. Richards, *The Word Bible Handbook*. Waco: Word, 1982.

You may wish to explore other handbooks and related literature recently published:

J. Robert Teringo, *The Land and People Jesus Knew: A Visual Tour of First-Century Palestine*. Minneapolis: Bethany 1985.

E. M. Blaiklock, *Today's Handbook of Bible Characters*. Minneapolis, 1979.

W. L. Coleman, *Today's Handbook of Bible Times & Customs*. Minneapolis: Bethany, 1984.

R. Gower, *The New Manners & Customs of Bible Times*. Chicago: Moody, 1987.

V. Gilbert Beers. *The Victor Handbook of Bible Knowledge*. Wheaton: Victor, 1981.

Merrill F. Unger, ed., *The New Unger's Bible Handbook*. Chicago: Moody, 1984.

Walter A. Elwell, *Baker's Bible Handbook*. Grand Rapids: Baker, 1989.

Thompson's *Handbook of Life in Bible Times*. IVF, 1986.

Nelson's *Comfort Print Bible Handbook*. Nashville: Nelson, 1995.

See too, V. Hamilton, *Handbook on the Pentateuch*. Baker, 1982.

Eerdmans' Handbook to the Bible, 1973.

Allan A. Swenson, *Plants of the Bible*. NY: Carol Publishing Group, 1995.

David E. O'Brien, *Today's Handbook for Solving Bible Difficulties*. Minneapolis: Bethany House, 1990.

VIII. Commentaries:

30-46. William Barclay, *The Daily Study Bible*. Philadelphia: Westminster, n.d.

47-56. *The Beacon Bible Commentary*. Kansas City: Beacon Hill, 1964-69.

57. Donald Guthrie, J.A. Motyer, A.M. Stibbs, D.J. Wiseman, eds. *The New Bible Commentary Revised.* Grand Rapids: Eerdmans, 1970.

Leander Keck *et al*, eds., *The New Interpreter's Bible.* Nashville: Abingdon, 1994 ff.

58. F.F. Bruce, *The International Bible Commentary* (N.I.V. text). Zondervan, 1986.

G. Roger Schoenhals, ed., *John Wesley's Commentary on the Bible: A One Volume Condensation of His Explanatory Notes.* Grand Rapids: Francis Asbury, 1990.

Anchor Bible Commentary (Garden City: Doubleday, 1965ff).

Eugene Carpenter and Wayne McCown, *The Asbury Commentary.* Grand Rapids: Zondervan, 1992.

C.W. Carter, ed., *The Wesleyan Bible Commentary.* 7 vols. Grand Rapids: Eerdmans, 1964-9.

59. F F. Bruce, *Commentary on the Book of the Acts: The English Text with Introduction, Exposition and Notes.* Grand Rapids: Eerdmans, 1955. (New International Commentary)

60. William Temple, *Readings in St. John's Gospel.* New York: Macmillan, 1945.

Stephen Neill, *The Christian Character.* London: Lutterworth, 1955.

61. Lloyd J. Ogilvie, general ed., *The Communicator's Commentary.* Waco: Word, 1980 ff. (a multi-volume work).

You should also consider *The Expositor's Bible Commentary* edited by Frank Gaebelein, a multi-volume work. Grand Rapids: Zondervan, 1979ff.

The Bible Background Commentary Downers Grove: IVP, 1993, 1997. Gives cultural context.

James Luther Mays, Ed., *Interpretation: A Bible Commentary for Teaching and Preaching.* Atlanta: John Knox Press, 1980's. A multi-volume work.

For extended help on biblical matters, including commentaries see *Biblical Resources For Ministry*. D.R. Bauer (Nappanee, IN,: Evangel, 1995).

IX. Supplementary Aids: (1) Biography and Church History:

62. J. D. Douglas, ed., *The New International Dictionary of the Christian Church*. rev. ed. Grand Rapids: Zondervan, 1978.

N.M.S. Cameron, ed., *Dictionary of Scottish Church History and Theology*. Downers Grove, IL: IVP 1993.

63. Tim Dowley, organizing ed., *Eerdmans' Handbook to the History of Christianity*. Grand Rapids: Eerdmans, 1977.

Mark Noll, Nathan O. Hatch, George M. Marsden, David F. Wells, John D. Woodbridge, eds., *Eerdmans' Handbook to Christianity in America*. Grand Rapids: Eerdmans, 1983.

Eerdmans' Handbook of Christianity in Today's World. Grand Rapids: Eerdmans, 1985.

64. Tony Lane, *Harper's Concise Book of Christian Faith*. New York: Harper and Brothers, 1984.

Larousse Biographical Dictionary, New York.: Larousse, 1990.

Merriam-Webster's Biographical Dictionary, 1995.

Larousse Biographical Dictionary, 5th ed. New York: Larousse, 1990.

Edith Dean, *All the Women of the Bible*. San Francisco: Harper Collins, 1988.

X. Supplementary Aids: (2) English Language Dictionaries and Writing Helps:

65-66. *Oxford English Dictionary*. New York: Oxford, 1989, micrographic printing in two volumes. (Compact and Revised edition 1991; regular edition in 20 volumes.)

67. *Random House Webster's Unabridged Dictionary*, 1999.

The Random House Dictionary of the English Language. 2nd ed. New York: Random House, 1998.

68. *Merriam-Webster's Collegiate* (latest edition—updated annually).

69. A synonym finder. Perhaps the best of the lot is *Rodale's Synonym Finder*, revision eds. Lawrence Urdang and Nancy LaRoche. Emmaus, PA: Rodale Press, 1986.

Compare *Merriam-Webster's Collegiate Thesaurus*, 1976.

70. William Strunk Jr. and E.B. White, *Elements of Style*. New York: Macmillan, 1999.

Tom McArthur, ed. *The Oxford Companion to the English Language*. New York: Oxford, 1992.

XI. Supplemental Aids: (3) Miscellaneous Reference Works that Provide Information and Resource for the Preacher:

71. Rodney J. Hunter, gen. ed., *Dictionary of Pastoral Care and Counseling*. Nashville: Abingdon, 1990.

Ralph G. Turnbull, ed. *Baker's Dictionary of Practical Theology*. Grand Rapids: Baker, 1967.

72. Richard J. Foster, *The Works of Richard Foster*. San Francisco: Harper, n.d. None better for clergy spiritual formation.

73-74. John Julian, *Dictionary of Hymnology*. 2 vols. Grand Rapids: Kregel, 1985.

75. Sherwood Eliot Wirt and Kersten Beckstrom, *Topical Encyclopedia of Living Quotations*. Minneapolis: Bethany House Publishers, 1982.

William Neil, comp., *Concise Dictionary of Religious Quotations*. London: Mobrays, 1975.

76. *The Oxford Dictionary of Quotations*. 5th ed. New York: Oxford, 1999.

Random House Webster's Quotationary, 1999.

Chambers, 1998.

Bartlett's, 1992.

The Book of Positive Quotations, 1997.

77. Alan Bullock and Oliver Stallybrass, *The Harper Dictionary of Modern Thought.* New York: Harper, 1977.

78. *The Concise Columbia Desk Encyclopedia,* 4th ed., 1994.

The Columbia Encyclopedia, 6th ed., 2000.

XII. Preaching, Homiletics, Etc.:

79-83. *20 Centuries of Great Preaching,* Clyde E.E. Fant Jr. and William M. Pinson, Jr., eds., Waco: Word, 1971. Especially helpful for its multiple index system.

For illustrations, see Paul Tan, *Encyclopedia of 7700 Illustrations.* Rockville, MD.: Assurance, 1979.

William H. Willimon and Richard Lischer, eds., *Concise Encyclopedia of Preaching.* Louisville: Westminster John Knox Press, 1995.

84. John Stott, *Between Two Worlds: The Art of Preaching in the 20th Century.* Grand Rapids: Eerdmans, 1982.

Harold T. Bryson, *Expository Preaching: The Art of Preaching Through A Book of the Bible.* Nashville: Broadman & Holman Publishers, 1995.

85. Haddon Robinson, *Biblical Preaching: The Development and Delivery of Expository Messages.* Grand Rapids: Baker, 1980.

86. Thomas Long, *The Senses of Preaching.* Atlanta: Knox, 1988.

Thomas Long, *The Witness of Preaching.* Louisville: Westminster John Knox, 1989.

George E. Sweazey, *Preaching the Good News.* Englewood Cliffs, NJ: Prentice-Hall, 1976.

87. James S. Stewart, *Heralds of God.* Grand Rapids: Baker, 1972.

James S. Stewart, *A Faith to Proclaim.* Grand Rapids: Baker, n.d.

James S. Stewart, *Thine is the Kingdom.* Edinburgh: St. Andrew, 1956.

James S. Stewart, *Exposition and Encounters: Preaching in the Context of Worship.* Mosley Road: Friends Institute, 1956.

See Stewart's homiletics worked out in his sermons, as in *Walking with God*. Gordon Grant, Ed., Edinburgh: St. Andrews, 1996.

88-89. Own at least two of J.S. Stewart's books of sermons, such as *River of Life*. Nashville: Abingdon, 1972; *Wind of the Spirit*. Grand Rapids: Baker, 1984; *Walking with God*. Grand Rapids: Baker, 1996.

90. P.T. Forsyth, *Positive Preaching and the Modern Mind*. Foreword by Ralph G. Turnbull. Grand Rapids: Baker, 1980.

James M. Black, *The Mystery of Preaching*. Old Tappan: Revell, 1934.

91. St. Augustine, *De Doctrina Christiana* [*Of Christian Doctrine*]. Book IV on preaching was the first homiletics textbook. Many editions.

92. Ralph G. Turnbull, *A History of Preaching: Volume 3*. Grand Rapids: Baker, 1974.

Cp. D.L. Larsen, *The Company of the Preachers: A History of Biblical Preaching From the O.T. to the Modern Era*. Grand Rapids: Kregel, 1998.

93. James D. Engel, *Contemporary Christian Communication: Its Theory and Practice*. Nashville: Nelson, 1979.

Calvin Miller, *The Empowered Communicator: 7 Keys to Unlocking an Audience*. Nashville: Broadman & Holman, 1994.

Calvin Miller, *Spirit, Word, and Story: A Philosophy of Marketplace Preaching*. Grand Rapids: Baker, 1997.

Raymond Bailey, ed., *Hermeneutics for Preaching: Approaches to Contemporary Interpretations of Scripture*. Nashville: Broadman Press, 1992.

George L. Klein, ed., *Reclaiming the Prophetic Mantle: Preaching the Old Testament Faithfully*. Nashville: Broadman Press, 1992.

Al Fasol, *With A Bible in Their Hands: Baptist Preaching in the South (1679–1979)*. Nashville: Broadman & Holman, 1994.

Raymond Bailey, *Jesus The Preacher*. Nashville: Broadman Press, 1990.

Raymond Bailey, *Paul The Preacher*. Nashville: Broadman Press, 1991.

94. W. E. Sangster, *The Craft of the Sermon*. London: Epworth, 1968.

Edward Markquart, *Quest For Better Preaching*. Augsburg, 1985.

David Buttrick, *Homiletic: Moves and Structures*. Philadelphia: Fortress Press, 1987.

Donald L. Hamilton, *Homiletic Handbook*. Nashville: Broadman Press, 1992.

Michael Duduit, ed., *Handbook of Contemporary Preaching*. Nashville: Broadman Press, 1992.

Michael Duduit, ed., *Communicate With Power: Insights from America's Top Communicators*. Grand Rapids: Baker, 1997.

Wayne McDill, *The 12 Essential Skills for Great Preaching*. Nashville: Broadman & Holman Publishers, 1994.

James D. Berkley, Gen. Ed., *Leadership Handbooks of Practical Theology*, Volume 1. Grand Rapids: Baker, 1992.

95. On inductive theory see Ralph L. Lewis and Gregg Lewis, *Inductive Preaching: Helping People Listen*. Westchester, IL: Crossway, 1983.

Ralph L. Lewis, *Inductive Preaching: Activities Guidebook*. Wilmore, KY: Creative Impressions, Inc., 1983. (Companion to *Inductive Preaching* above.)

Fred Craddock, *Preaching*. Nashville: Abingdon, 1989.

Elizabeth Achtemeier, *Creative Preaching: Finding the Words*. Nashville: Abingdon, 1980.

Edward K. Rowell, ed., *Fresh Illustrations for Preaching and Teaching from Leadership Journal*. Grand Rapids: Baker, 1997.

96. J. H. Jowett, *The Preacher: His Life and Work*. Grand Rapids: Baker, 1968.

Phillips Brooks, *On Preaching*. London: S.P.C.K.: 1965.

97. James W. Cox, ed., *Biblical Preaching: An Expositor's Treasury*. Philadelphia: Westminster, 1983.

Richard Baxter, *The Reformed Pastor*. Multnomah, 1982.

Cp. *The Protestant Pulpit* anthology edited by Andrew Blackwood. Abingdon, 1947 (reprinted by Baker). See also other anthologies of sermons (e.g. those done by J. Cox).

98. Donald G. Miller, *The Way to Biblical Preaching: How to Communicate the Gospel in Depth.* Nashville: Abingdon, 1957. Also see his *Fire in Thy Mouth.* Baker reprint, 1976.

99. James S. Stewart, *A Man in Christ,* 1935. Best for theological basis of preaching message.

FOR MORE BIBLIOGRAPHY ON PREACHING:

100. William Toohey, and William Thompson, editors, *Recent Homiletical Thought: A Bibliography,* 1935–65. Nashville: Abingdon, 1967.

A. Duane Litfin and Haddon W. Robinson, editors, *Recent Homiletical Thought: An Annotated Bibliography, Volume 2, 1966-1979.* Grand Rapids: Baker, 1983.

Batsell Barrett Baxter, *Heart of Yale Lectures.* Macmillan, 1947.

C.J. Barber's *The Minister's Library.* Baker: vols. 1, 2 1985 and 1987. You may also wish to see Barber's other books in this bibliographical series.

Donald E. Demaray, *Introduction to Homiletics* (2nd Ed., 1990) with bibliographies at close of chapters and a more extensive bibliography at the end of the book.

See also Bibliography to this book, *Proclaiming the Truth.*

*For more information on other resources see:

David R. Bauer, *Biblical Resources for Ministry: A Bibliography of Works in Biblical Studies.* 2nd Ed. Nappanee, IN: Evangel Publishing House, 1995. Dr. Bauer includes Bible Software Programs, pp. 131ff.

Do not overlook the *Leadership* journal resources for illustrations and sermon ideas: www.PreachingToday.com

BIBLIOGRAPHY

Adler, Mortimer J., and Martin L. Gross. "Conversation with an Author: Dr. Mortimer J. Adler, Philosopher and Author of *Aristotle for Everybody*." *Book Digest*, May 1978, 19-32.

Advices and Queries: Addressed to the Meetings and Members of the Religious Society of Friends, and to Those Who Meet with Them in Public Worship. London: The Society of Friends, 1964.

Allmen, J.J. von. *Preaching and Congregation*. London: Lutterworth Press, n.d.

————, ed. *Vocabulary of the Bible*. London: Lutterworth Press, 1958.

Aristotle. *On Rhetoric*. Newly trans. by George A. Kennedy. New York: Oxford, 1991.

Arnett, William M. "John Wesley and the Bible." *Wesleyan Theological Journal*, Spring 1968, 3-9.

Augustine, Saint. *On Christian Doctrine*. Translated with an introduction by D.W. Robertson, Jr. Indianapolis: Bobbs-Merrill, 1958.

Bailey, Raymond, ed. *Hermeneutics for Preaching: Approaches to Contemporary Interpretations of Scripture*. Nashville: Broadman, 1992.

Bainton, Roland H. *Here I Stand*. Nashville: Abingdon, 1951.

Barclay, William. *Daily Celebration*. vol. 2. Waco, TX: Word, 1973.

————. *The Master's Men*. Nashville: Abingdon, 1976.

_____. *William Barclay: A Spiritual Autobiography.* Grand Rapids: William B. Eerdmans, 1975.

Barth, Karl. *Prayer and Preaching.* Translated by S. F. Terrien. Translation revised by B. E. Hooke. London: SCM Press, 1964.

————. *The Preaching of the Gospel.* Translated by. B.E. Hooke. Philadelphia: Westminster, 1963.

Bastian, Donald N. "Interview with Bishop Bastian." *Light and Life*, 20 June 1978, 6-9.

Baxter, Batsell Barrett. *The Heart of the Yale Lectures.* Grand Rapids: Baker Book House, 1971 reprint.

Berkley, James D., ed. *Leadership Handbooks of Practical Theology*, vol. 1. Grand Rapids: Baker, 1992.

Black, James. *The Mystery of Preaching.* London: James Clarke & Company, Ltd. 1934. Note the new edition by Peter Cotterell (London: Marshall, Morgan and Scott, 1977) and the Zondervan reprint (Grand Rapids, 1978).

Blackwood, Andrew W. *Expository Preaching for Today: Case Studies of Bible Passages.* Grand Rapids: Baker Book House, 1975 reprint.

————. *Preaching from Samuel.* Grand Rapids: Baker Book House, 1975 reprint.

————, compiler. *The Protestant Pulpit: An Anthology of Master Sermons from the Reformation to Our Own Day.* Nashville: Abingdon, 1974.

Bowie, Walter Russell. *Learning to Live.* Nashville: Abingdon, 1969.

Braaten, Carl E. *New Directions in Theology Today: History and Hermeneutics.* vol. 2. Philadelphia: Westminster Press, 1966.

Bradley, Bert E. *Fundamentals of Speech Communication: The Credibility of Ideas.* Dubuque, IA: Wm. C. Brown Co., 1974.

Brooks, Phillips. *The Light of the World and Other Sermons*. New York: E. P. Dutton & Company, 1890.

Brown, H. C., Jr., H. Gordon Clinard, Jesse J. Northcutt, and Al Fasol. *Steps to the Sermon: An Eight-Step Plan for Preaching with Confidence*. Nashville: Broadman, 1996.

Bruce, F. F. "Are the New Testament Documents Still Reliable?" *Christianity Today*, 20 October 1978, 28-33.

———. *The New Testament Documents: Are They Reliable?* Grand Rapids: William B. Eerdmans, 1959.

Burghardt, Walter J. *Preaching, the Art and the Craft*. New York: Paulist, 1987.

Buttrick, David. *Homiletic: Moves and Structures*. Philadelphia: Fortress, 1987.

Caine, Lynn. *Lifelines*. New York: Doubleday, 1977.

Cassels, Louis. "A Consumer of Sermonology Speaks Out." *Christian Herald*, April 1974, 26-29.

Christian Faith and Practice in the Experience of the Society of Friends. London: Yearly Meeting of the Religious Society of Friends, 1960.

Christianity Today. 12 June 2000, the issue on use of money.

Clark, Glenn. *Health Through Prayer*. Evesham, England: Arthur James, 1955; New York: Harper & Row, 1977 reprint.

Clark, I. W. "My Pastor's Preaching." *The Preacher's Magazine*, February 1973, 22.

Classics Devotional Bible. Grand Rapids: Zondervan, 1996.

Coker, William B. "Prophetic Succession." *The Asbury Seminarian*, January 1970, 3-6.

Coleman, William L. "Billy Sunday: A Style Meant for His Time and Place." *Christianity Today*, 17 December 1976, 14-17.

Coote, Algerton C. P. *The Preacher's Homiletic Helper*. Grand Rapids: Baker Book House, 1975 reprint.

Cowan, Arthur A. *The Primacy of Preaching Today: The Warrack Lectures for 1954*. Edinburgh: T. & T. Clark, 1955.

Cox, James W., ed., *Biblical Preaching: An Expositor's Treasury*. Philadelphia: Westminster, 1983.

Cox, James W. "'Eloquent, Mighty in the Scriptures': Biblical Preaching from Chrysostom to Thielicke," *Review and Expositor*, Spring 1975, 189-201.

———. *A Guide to Biblical Preaching*. Nashville: Abingdon, 1976.

Craddock, Fred B. *Preaching*. Nashville: Abingdon, 1985.

———. *As One Without Authority*. Nashville: Abingdon, 1979.

Daane, James. *Preaching with Confidence: A Theological Essay on the Power of the Pulpit*. Grand Rapids: Eerdmans, 1980.

Davis, Henry Grady. *Design for Preaching*. Philadelphia: Fortress, 1958.

Dayton, Donald W. *Discovering an Evangelical Heritage*. New York: Harper & Row, 1976.

Demaray, Donald E. *Introduction to Homiletics*. Indianapolis: Light and Life, 1990 (2d ed.).

Doberstein, John W., ed. *Minister's Prayer Book: An Order of Prayers and Readings*. Philadelphia: Fortress Press, n.d.

"A Dozen Bibles: A Survey." *Christianity Today*, 20 October 1978, 20-22.

Drakeford, John W. *Humor in Preaching*. Grand Rapids: Zondervan (Ministry Resources Library), 1986.

Duduit, Michael, ed., *Handbook of Contemporary Preaching*. Nashville: Broadman Press, 1992.

Duke, Robert W. *The Sermon as God's Word: Theologies for Preaching*. Nashville; Abingdon, 1980.

Edelhart, Mike. "Passing the Stress Test." *Atlanta*, December 1978, 122ff.

Engel, James F. *Contemporary Christian Communications: Its Theory and Practice*. Nashville: Nelson, 1975.

Eslinger, Richard L. *Pitfalls in Preaching*. Grand Rapids: Eerdmans, 1996.

Evangelism Alert: Official Reference Volume, European Congress on Evangelism, Amsterdam, 1971. Edited by Gilbert W. Kirby. London: World Wide Publications, 1972.

Fasol, Al. *Essentials for Biblical Preaching*. Grand Rapids: Baker, 1989.

———. *With a Bible in Their Hands: Baptist Preaching in the South 1679-1979*. Nashville: Broadman, 1994.

Fast, Julius. *Body Language*. New York: M. Evans and Co., Inc., 1970.

Findlay, James F., Jr. *Dwight L. Moody: American Evangelist, 1837-1899*. Chicago: University of Chicago Press, 1969.

Flesch, Rudolf. *The Art of Clear Thinking*. New York: Collier, 1971 (7th printing).

———. *The Art of Plain Talk*. New York: Collier, 1971 (6th printing).

Fletcher, Joseph. *Situation Ethics*. Philadelphia: Westminster Press, 1966.

Foster, Richard J. and Emilie Griffin, *Spiritual Classics: Selected Readings for Individuals and Groups on the Twelve Spiritual Disciplines*. San Francisco: Harper, 2000.

———. *Celebration of Discipline: The Path to Spiritual Growth*. Revised ed. San Francisco: Harper, 1988.

————. *The Challenge of the Disciplined Life* (formerly *Money, Sex and Power*). San Francisco: Harper, 1st ed. 1985.

————. *Prayer: Finding the Heart's True Home*. San Francisco: Harper, 1992.

————. *Streams of Living Water: Celebrating the Great Traditions of Christian Faith*. San Francisco: Harper, 1998.

———— and James Bryan Smith. *Devotional Classics: Selected Readings for Individuals and Groups*. San Francisco: Harper, 1993.

Freeman, Harold. *Variety in Biblical Preaching: Innovative Techniques and Fresh Forms*. Waco: Word, 1987.

Garrison, Webb B. *Taking the Drudgery out of Sermon Preparation*. Grand Rapids: Baker Book House, 1975 reprint.

Gibson, George Miles. *Planned Preaching*. Philadelphia: Westminster, 1954.

Goldingway, C. John. "Expounding the New Testament." In *New Testament Interpretation*, edited by I. Howard Marshall, 351-65. Exeter: Paternoster Press, 1977.

Gossip, A. J. *Experience Worketh Hope: Being Some Thoughts for a Troubled Day*. Edinburgh: T. and T. Clark, 1945.

Graham, Billy. "Biblical Authority in Evangelism." *Christianity Today*, 15 October 1956, 5.

Great Preaching: Evangelical Messages by Contemporary Christians. Edited by Sherwood Eliot Wirt and Viola Blake. Waco, TX: Word Books, 1963.

Gregory of Nyssa. *The Life of Moses*. Translated and edited by Abraham J. Malherbe and Everett Ferguson. New York: Paulist Press, 1978.

Griffith, A. Leonard. *The Need to Preach*. London: Hodder and Stoughton, 1971.

Gross, John, ed., *The Oxford Book of Essays*. New York: Oxford, 1991.

Gross, Martin L. *The Psychological Society*. New York: Random House, 1978.

Gundry, Stanley N. "Grand Themes of D. L. Moody." *Christianity Today*, 20 December 1974, 4-6.

Hamilton, Donald L. *Homiletical Handbook*. Nashville: Broadman, 1992.

The Harper Dictionary of Modern Thought. Edited by Alan Bullock and Oliver Stallybrass. New York: Harper & Row, 1977.

Hartley, John E. "Hermeneutical Principles Relevant to the Two Testaments." *The Asbury Seminarian*, April 1968, 19-27.

Hayakawa, S. E., ed. *The Use and Misuse of Language*. Greenwich, CT: Fawcett Publications, Inc., 1962.

Heisey, D. Ray. "The Warrack Lectures on Preaching." *Preaching: A Journal of Homiletics*, vol.1, no.8 (1966), 5-14.

Hines, John R. "The Decline of the Sower: A Modest Critique of the Preaching Role." No.1 of the Sprigg Lectures for 1976. *Virginia Seminary Journal*, February 1977.

Holland, DeWitte T. *The Preaching Tradition: A Brief History*. Nashville: Abingdon, 1980.

———. *Preaching in American History*. Nashville, Abingdon, 1969.

Hostetler, Michael J. *Introducing the Sermon: The Art of Compelling Beginnings*. Grand Rapids: Zondervan (Ministry Resources Library), 1986.

Howe, Reuel L. *The Miracle of Dialogue*. New York: Seabury, 1963.

Huck-Lietzmann, *Gospel Parallels: A Synopsis of the First Three Gospels*. New York: Nelson, 1949.

Jabusch, Willard F. *The Person in the Pulpit: Preaching as Caring*. Nashville: Abingdon, 1980.

Jones, E. Stanley. *The Divine Yes*. Nashville: Abingdon, 1975.

Jones, Peter Rhea. "Biblical Hermeneutics." *Review and Expositor*, Spring 1975, 139.

Jowett, J. H. *The Preacher: His Life and Work*. Grand Rapids: Baker, 1968 reprint.

Keck, Leander. *The Bible in the Pulpit: The Renewal of Biblical Preaching*. Nashville: Abingdon, 1978.

Keener, Craig S. *The IVP Bible Background Commentary: New Testament*. Downers Grove: IVP, 1993.

Killinger, John. *The Word Not Bound*. Waco: Word, 1967.

Kinlaw, Dennis F. *Preaching in the Spirit*. Grand Rapids: Francis Asbury, 1985.

Korda, Michael. *Success! How Every Man and Woman Can Achieve It*. New York: Random House, 1977; condensed in *Book Digest*, August 1978, 154-74.

Kraemer, Hendrik. *The Communication of the Christian Faith*. Philadelphia: Westminster Press, 1956; London: Lutterworth Press, 1957.

Ladd, George E. *I Believe in the Resurrection*. London: Hodder and Stoughton, 1975; Grand Rapids: William B. Eerdmans, 1975.

Larsen, David L. *The Company of the Preachers: A History of Biblical Preaching from the Old Testament to the Modern Era*. Grand Rapids: Kregel, 1998.

Lewis, Ralph L. "Four Preaching Aims of Amos." *The Asbury Seminarian*, April 1967, 14-18.

———, with Greg Lewis. *Inductive Preaching: Helping People Listen*. Westchester, IL: Crossway, 1983.

———. *Learning to Preach Like Jesus*. Westchester, IL: Crossway Books, 1989.

———. *Persuasive Preaching Today*. Wilmore, KY: Asbury Theological Seminary, 1977.

Lindsell, Harold. *When You Pray*. Grand Rapids: Baker Book House, 1969.

Lischer, Richard. *Theories of Preaching: Selected Readings in the Homiletical Tradition*. Durham, NC: Labyrinth Press, 1987.

Lloyd-Jones, D. Martyn. *Preaching and Preachers*. Grand Rapids: Zondervan, 1971.

———. *Romans: An Exposition of Chapter 8:17-39, The Final Perseverance of the Saints*. Grand Rapids: Zondervan, 1976.

Long, Thomas C. *The Senses of Preaching*. Atlanta: John Knox, 1988.

———. *The Witness of Preaching*. Louisville: Westminster: John Knox, 1989.

Lowry, Eugene L. *How to Preface a Parable: Designs for Narrative Sermons*. Nashville: Abingdon, 1989.

Luther, Darrell E. "Making Life-Situation Preaching Biblical." In *Biblical Preaching for Contemporary Man*, compiled by Neil B. Wiseman, 119-33. Grand Rapids: Baker Book House, 1977.

McCracken, Robert J. *The Making of the Sermon*. London: SCM Press, 1956; New York: Harper & Row, 1956.

McCumber, W. E., ed. *Holiness Preachers and Preaching*. Kansas City: Beacon, 1989. (Volume 9 of *Great Holiness Classics*).

McPhee, John. *Coming into the Country*. New York: Farrar, Straus & Giroux, 1977.

Macpherson, Ian. *The Burden of the Lord: Lectures on Preaching*. London: The Epworth Press, 1953; Nashville: Abingdon, 1955.

Markquart, Edward F. *Quest for Better Preaching: Resources for Renewal in the Pulpit*. Minneapolis: Augsburg, 1985.

Marshall, I. Howard, ed. *New Testament Interpretation*. Exeter: Paternoster, 1977.

Massey, James Earl. *The Sermon in Perspective: A Study of Communication and Charisma*. Grand Rapids: Baker, 1976.

Mavis, W. Curry. *The Holy Spirit in the Christian Life*. Grand Rapids: Baker Book House, 1977.

Mehrabian, Albert. *Silent Messages*. Belmont, CA: Wadsworth Publishing Company, Inc., 1971.

Miller, Calvin. *Spirit, Word, and Story: A Philosophy of Marketplace Preaching*. Grand Rapids: Baker, 1996.

———. *The Empowered Communicator (7 Keys to Unlocking an Audience)*. Nashville: Broadman and Holeman, 1994.

Miller, Donald G. *Fire in Thy Mouth*. Grand Rapids: Baker Book House, 1976 reprint.

———. *The Way to Biblical Preaching*. Nashville: Abingdon, 1957; paperback, 1974.

Monroe, Alan H., and Ehringer, Douglas. *Principles of Speech Communication*. 7th ed. Glenview, IL: Scott, Foresman and Company, 1975.

Morgan, G. Campbell. *Preaching*. London: Marshall, Morgan and Scott, Ltd., 1937.

Morgan, Ted. *On Becoming American*. Boston: Houghton Mifflin Company, 1978; condensed in *Book Digest*, August 1978, 130-53.

Morris, Colin. *The Word and the Words*. Nashville: Abingdon, 1975.

Mounce, Robert H. *The Essential Nature of New Testament Preaching*. Grand Rapids: William B. Eerdmans, 1960.

Neill, Stephen. *The Christian Character*. London: Lutterworth Press, 1955.

The New International Dictionary of New Testament Theology. 3 vols. Edited by Colin Brown. Grand Rapids: Zondervan, 1978.

Newman, John Henry. *The Idea of a University*. Oxford: Clarendon Press, 1976 reprint.

Norris, Kathleen. *Amazing Grace: A Vocabulary of Faith*. New York: Riverhead, 1998.

Olford, Stephen E. with David L. Olford. *Anointed Expository Preaching*. Nashville: Broadman, 1998.

The Oxford Book of Literary Anecdotes. Edited by James Sutherland. Oxford and London: Oxford University Press, 1975.

The Penguin Dictionary of Quotations. Edited by J. M. and M. J. Cohen. New York: Penguin Books, 1960.

Perry, Lloyd M. *Biblical Preaching for Today's World*. Chicago: Moody Press, 1973.

Philip, James, George M. Philip, and William Still. *Review of the Ministry: Its Ethos, Practice and Goals*. Aberdeen, Scotland:1989.

Potter, G. R. *Zwingli*. New York: Cambridge University Press, 1976.

Read, David H. C. *Sent from God: The Enduring Power and Mystery of Preaching*. Nashville: Abingdon, 1974.

Recent Homiletical Thought: A Bibliography, 1935-1965. Edited by William Toohey and William D. Thompson. Nashville: Abingdon, 1967.

Recent Homiletical Thought: A Bibliography, vol. 2, 1966-1979. Grand Rapids: Baker, 1983.

Reflecting God Study Bible. Kenneth Barker, gen. ed. Grand Rapids: Zondervan, 2000.

Reu, M. *Homiletics: A Manual of the Theory and Practice of Preaching*. Translated by Albert Steinhaeuser. Grand Rapids: Baker Book House, 1967.

Robinson, Haddon W. *Biblical Preaching: The Development and Delivery of Expository Messages.* Grand Rapids: Baker, 1980.

Rowell, Edward K., *Preaching with Spiritual Passion.* Minneapolis: Bethany, 1998.

Rupert, Hoover. "Woe Is Me, If I Preach Not…!" *The Sermon Builder*, June 1976, 5ff.

Ryken, Leland. *The Literature of the Bible.* Grand Rapids: Zondervan, 1974.

Saltmarsh, John. *King's College Chapel.* Norwich: Jarrold & Sons Ltd., 1971.

Scherer, Paul. *For We Have This Treasure: The Yale Lectures on Preaching for 1943.* Grand Rapids: Baker Book House, 1976 reprint.

———. *The Word of God Sent.* Grand Rapids: Baker Book House, 1977 reprint.

Scholer, David M. *A Basic Bibliographic Guide for New Testament Exegesis.* 2d ed. Grand Rapids: William B. Eerdmans, 1973.

Schuller, Robert H. *Reach Out for New Life.* New York: Hawthorn Books, 1977.

———. *Self-Love: The Dynamic Force of Success.* New York: Hawthorn Books, 1969.

Severance, W. Murray. *Pronouncing Bible Names.* Nashville: Broadman, 1994.

Shepard, Fred. "'So What?' Preparation." In *Innovative Ideas for Pastors*, compiled by Neil B. Wiseman, 19. Kansas City: Beacon Hill Press, 1976.

Sleeth, Ronald E. "The Crisis in Preaching." *The Perkins Journal*, Summer 1977, 2–41.

Smith, David. *The Art of Preaching.* New York: Doran, n.d.

Stanger, Frank Bateman. "The Healing Power of Love: What Better Medicine Is There?" *The Herald*, July/August 1978, 12ff.

Stewart, James S. *Heralds of God: The Warrack Lectures*. London: Hodder and Stoughton, 1946; Grand Rapids: Baker Book House, 1972 reprint.

———. *King For Ever*. Nashville: Abingdon, 1975.

———. *The Wind of the Spirit*. Nashville: Abingdon, 1968.

———. *Walking with God*. Edinburgh: St. Andrews Press, 1996.

Stott, John R. W. "Are Evangelicals Fundamentalists?" *Christianity Today*, 8 September 1978, 44-46.

———. *I Believe in Preaching*. London: Hodder and Stoughton, 1982. Printed in the U.S. by Eerdmans as *Between Two Worlds*.

———. *The Preacher's Portrait: Some New Testament Word Studies*. London: Tyndale Press, 1961; Grand Rapids: William B. Eerdmans, 1964.

———, ed. *Obeying Christ in a Changing World: The Lord Christ*. vol.1. Glasgow: Wm. Collins Sons & Co., 1977.

Strait, C. Neil. "Give Them Hope." *The Preacher's Magazine*, April 1973, 5.

Stuhlmacher, Peter. "Adolf Schlatter's Interpretation of Scripture." *New Testament Studies* (Cambridge), July 1978, 433-36.

Sweazey, George E. *Preaching the Good News*. Englewood Cliffs, NJ: Prentice-Hall, 1976.

Telford, John. *The Life of John Wesley*. London: The Epworth Press, 1960 reprint.

"The Story of M. S. Scott." *Decision*, August 1978, 11.

Thomas, Dylan. *Poet in the Making: The Notebooks of Dylan Thomas*. Edited by Ralph Maud. London: J. M. Dent and Sons, Ltd., 1965.

Thonssen, Lester and A. Craig Baird. *Speech Criticism: The Development of Standards for Rhetorical Appraisal.* New York: Ronald, 1948.

Torry, Peter. "The Mystery and Power of Preaching." *Christianity Today*, 22 September 1978, 30-31.

Traina, Robert A. *Methodical Bible Study.* Wilmore, KY: Robert A. Traina, 1952.

————. "The 'New Hermeneutic.'" *The Asbury Seminarian*, April 1967, 26-30.

Trueblood, Elton. *The Meditations of Elton Trueblood.* Edited by Stephen R. Sebert and W. Gordon Ross. New York: Harper & Row, 1975.

Turnbull, Ralph G. *A History of Preaching.* vol. 3. Grand Rapids: Baker Book House, 1974.

————, ed. *Baker's Dictionary of Practical Theology.* Grand Rapids: Baker Book House, 1967.

Turner, George A. "The Interpreter's Task." *The Asbury Seminarian*, April 1968, 3-7.

Twenty Centuries of Great Preaching: An Encyclopedia of Preaching. Edited by Clyde E. Fant, Jr., and William M. Pinson, Jr. Thirteen volumes. Waco, TX: Word Books, 1971.

Underhill, Evelyn. *The Spiritual Life.* New York: Harper & Row, n.d.

Walton, John H. and Victor Matthews. *The IVP Bible Background Commentary: Genesis-Deuteronomy.* Downers Grove: IVP, 1997.

Wesley, John. *The Letters of the Rev. John Wesley, A.M.* vol.2. Edited by John Telford. London: The Epworth Press, 1931.

White, Robert J. "Thoughts of a Brain Surgeon." *Reader's Digest*, September 1978, 97-100.

Wiersbe, Warren W. *Preaching and Teaching with Imagination: The Quest for Biblical Ministry*. Wheaton: Victor, 1994.

———. *Walking with the Giants*. Grand Rapids: Baker Book House, 1976.

Willard, Dallas. *The Divine Conspiracy: Rediscovering Our Hidden Life in God*. San Francisco: Harper, 1998.

Willimon, William H. and Richard Lischer, eds. *Concise Encyclopedia of Preaching*. Louisville: Westminster, 1995.

Wilson, Paul Scott. *The Four Pages of the Sermon: A Guide to Biblical Preaching*. Nashville: Abingdon, 1999.

Wiseman, Neil B., comp. *Biblical Preaching for Contemporary Man*. Grand Rapids: Baker Book House, 1977.

———. *Innovative Ideas for Pastors*. Kansas City: Beacon Hill Press, 1976.

.

General Index

The Bibliography is not included in this Index.

Abstract expression, 65

Activeness in speech, 70

Apropos language, 67

Atlases, Bible, 90

Audience reaction, 35

Authority, 16, 42, 73-74, 77-78, 80-84; Spirit as provider of, 78-80

Belief, 16, 19, 29, 42, 66, 84

Bible: authority of, 81, 83; as center of preaching, 25; versions of, 85

Bibliographical resources, 98

Biography, books of, 93

Body language. *See* Kinesics

Brain (left brain, right brain), 5-8

Character, 26, 74, 84

Christ, 16, 55, 82; as focal point of interpretation of Scripture, 48-49

Church as authorizer of preacher, 80

Church history, books on, 93

Church setting as determinant of language, 67

Clarity, 13, 41, 64-65

Commentaries, 27, 48, 50, 91-93

Communication, 2, 13-14, 59, 64, 68, 73, 84

Compulsion, preaching by, 15-16

Concordances, 86-87

Context, determining, 46-47, 84

Conviction, preaching by, 16-17, 49, 69

Creeds, 25-26

Dedication, 74-75, 84

Defining terms, 44, 66

Delivery, 11, 31-32, 84

Dictionaries: Bible, 88-90; English language, 11; theological, 34-35

Didache, 28-30

Economic language, 67-68

Efficient language, 68

Empathy with congregation, 75-76, 84. *See also* Needs, preaching to meet human

Emphasis, proper, 9, 54, 76-77, 84

Encyclopedias, Bible, 88-90

Experience, preaching from, 17-18, 50

Eye contact, 13-14, 77

Focus, 2, 12-13, 46

Genre, identifying literary, 44

Geography, books on, 48, 90-91

Grammar, 9-11, 63

Handbooks, 90-91

Harmonies, Gospel, 87

Holy Spirit, 25, 50, 52, 78, 80, 84

Homiletics, 2, 14; books on, 95-98

Homilia, 28, 30

Honesty, 37-38. *See also* Integrity

Illustrations, 6-8, 18, 50, 69-70

Imagination, 57

Individuality of style, 63

Integration, 53-71

Integrity, 10-11, 36, 38, 53
Intelligibility in preaching, 33-35
Interpretation, 39-51

Jargon, 66-67

Kerygma, 28-30
Kinesics, 2, 13-14, 77, 103

Language, 9-11, 35, 66-71, 83
Law, overemphasis on, 77
Learner, the preacher as, 31-33
Learning styles, 8-9
Lectio continua, 26
Lectionaries, 17, 26-28
Lectio selecta, 26-28
Lexicons, 87
Linguistics, *See* Language
Listening, importance of, 11-12
Loaded terms, 65

Meanings, determining, 39-52, 64-68
Monroe's motivational sequence, 60
Mood, 42, 67
Morality, implementation of (key to relevance), 36
Movement. *See* Kinesics
Music, books on, 94

Needs, preaching to meet human, 36
Neurolinguistic programming, 8
Notes, recording of, 40-43

Paraklesis, 28-30
Parallel passages, 45
Passage (Scripture) as determinant of language, 67
Personal, being (key to relevance), 35

Persons (clue to structure), 56-57
Persuasion, 60
Pictorial language, 4-8, 69, 71
Pictorializing, 4, 60
Pictures (clue to structure), 57-59
Place (clue to structure), 56
Posture, 13
Pragmatism, of Scripture, 81-83
Prayer, 6-7, 78-79, 84
Preaching, books on, 95-98
Precision in language, 9-11, 62-65
Present tense, 70
Proof-texting, 46

Quotations, 73-74; dictionaries of, 94-95

Reading, importance of, 10
Reference works, miscellaneous, 11, 94-95
Relevance in preaching, 30, 35-37, 50, 70
Repetition, 33, 68

Setting, 66-67, 82
Sincerity, 37-38. *See also* Integrity
Speech, 2, 16, 34-35, 67-71, 77-78. *See also* Language
Stewardship with words, 67-68, 71
Structure and structuring, 32, 53-61
Study procedures, 31-33. *See also* Interpretation
Style, 63, 68-69. *See also* Language
Subject check list, 19-24
Systematic preaching, 26-28

Teaching, preaching as, 28-31
Technique, 1-2, 14
Time (clue to structure), 53-55
Tonetics (tone), 2, 9, 12-13

Topical headings (clue to structure), 59-60
Transitions, 3-4, 61-63
Voice, 12-13

Witnesses, authoritative , 73-74
Word books (theological dictionaries, etc.), 88

Worksheet, 42-43, 46. *See also* Subject check list
Worship, 4-5, 37, 80
Writing out sermons, 2, 11, 50

Index of Persons

The Appendix and the Bibliography are not included in this Index.

Adler, Mortimer, 41n
Anderson, Norman H., 37
Augustine, 39

Bailey, A. Purnell, 49n
Bainton, Roland H., 31n
Barclay, William, xvii, 1, 15-17, 25-28, 30, 33-37, 51
Barlow, Charles L., 13n
Barr, James, 39n
Barth, Karl, 79n
Bartlett, David L., 73n
Bastian, Donald, 13
Baxter, Richard, xv
Beecher, Henry Ward, 81n
Black, James, 46n, 64
Blackwood, Andrew W., 27n
Blake, Viola , 70n
Blanton, Smiley, 81
Bradley, Bert E., 37, 67n
Broadus, John A., 15
Brooks, Phillip, 50

Cassels, Louis, 64n
Chrysostom, 48n
Cicero, 1
Clark, Glenn, 50n
Clark, Herbert H., 76
Coker, William B., 83n
Coote, Algerton C.P., 46n
Cox, James W., 46n, 48n, 69n
Craddock, Fred B., 69n

Dale, R.W., 82n
Doberstein, John W., 45n, 74n
Dorsey, Gary, 76
Duff, Mounstuart E. Grant, 33n

Ehringer, Douglas, 60n, 65n, 73n
Eliot, George, 50n

Fant, Clyde E., Jr., 80n
Ferguson, Everett, 48n
Findlay, James F., 69n
Foster, Richard, 10, 84n

Garrison, Webb B., 69, 73
Goldingway, C. John, 43n
Graham, Billy, xvi, 81-82
Gregory of Nyssa, 48n
Gundry, Stanley N., 78n

Harris, Joel Chandler, 50n
Hitler, Adolph, x

Irving, Washington, 10

James, William, 69n
Jennings, Peter, 11
Jones, Peter Rhea, 45n, 48n, 83n
Jowett, John Henry, 2n

Kennedy, D. James, 12
Kennedy, Earl, x n
Kennedy, Gerald, xii
Knox, John, 83n
Korda, Michael, 76n
Kraemer, Hendrick, 29n

Lewis, C.S., 10
Lewis, Ralph L., 69n, 81n
Lindsell, Harold, 78n
Lischer, Richard, 15, 39n
Lloyd-Jones, D. Martyn, 27, 80n
Luther, Martin, 6, 31n, 45n, 81n, 83n
Lyons, Mary E., 63n

Malherbe, Abraham J., 48n
Marshall, I. Howard, 43n
Maurice, Frederick Denison, 33n
Mavis, W. Curry, 68n, 74
McClure, John S., 12n, 67n
McCracken, Robert J., 26n
Merton, Thomas, 10
Miller, Calvin, 51n

Miller, Donald C., 39n
Monroe, Alan H, 60, 65n, 73n
Moody, Dwight L., 63n, 69n 78n, 81
Morgan, G. Campbell, 82n
Morgan, Ted, 64n
Morris, Colin, 67n
Mounce, Robert, 28, 29n

Newman, John Henry, 49n, 50n
Nouwen, Henri, 10

Origen, 48n

Pinson, William M., Jr., 80n
Pope, Alexander, xvi
Potter, G.R., 27n

Quayle, William A., xiii

Ramm, Bernard, 39n
Read, David H.C., 1, 51n
Ricoeur, Paul, 40n
Robertson, A.T., 78n
Robertson, Don, 7
Ross, Gordon, 74n
Ryken, Leland, 45n

Saltmarsh, John, 53
Scherer, Paul, 73n
Schlatter, Adolf, 40n
Sebert, Stephen, 74n
Shakespeare, William, 77
Sheppard, Dick, 74n
Sleeth, Ronald E., 67n
Socrates, x, 50n
Spurgeon, Charles, 16, 48n
Stanger, Frank Bateman, 81n
Stevenson, Robert Louis, 69n
Stewart, James S., 68, 70n, 79
Stott, John R.W., 29n, 39n

Stuhlmacher, Peter, 40n
Sunday, Billy, 81
Sweazey, George E., 51n, 63n, 67n
Swindoll, Charles, 12, 70n

Telford, John, 63, 81n
Thielicke, Helmut, 48n
Thomas, Dylan, 70n
Tolkien, J.R.R., 10
Torry, Peter, 78n
Traina, Robert A., 39n, 46n
Trueblood, Elton, 74n

Turnbull, Ralph G., 39n
Turner, George A., 49n

von Allmen, J.J., 27n, 49n, 68n, 78n

Wesley, John, 35, 63n, 77n, 81n
White, Robert J., 78n
Wiersbe, Warren, 51n, 78n
Willard, Dallas, 10
Wirt, Sherwood Eliot, 70n
Wren, Christopher, 53

Zwingli, Huldreich, 27, 80n